30-MINUTE GROUPS

PEACEFUL CONFLICT RESOLUTION

STRENGTHENING COMMUNICATION SKILLS, FOSTERING COOPERATION, AND RESOLVING DISPUTES

AMIE DEAN

Duplication and Copyright

No part of this publication may be reproduced, stored in a retrieval system, or transmitted in any form by any means, electronic, mechanical, photocopy, video or audio recording, or otherwise without prior written permission from the publisher, except for all worksheets and activities which may be reproduced for a specific group or class. Reproduction for an entire school or school district is prohibited.

NCYI titles may be purchased in bulk at special discounts for educational, business, fundraising, or promotional use. For more information, please email sales@ncyi.org.

NATIONAL CENTER for YOUTH ISSUES
P.O. Box 22185
Chattanooga, TN 37422-2185
423.899.5714 • 866.318.6294
fax: 423.899.4547 • www.ncyi.org

ISBN: 9781965066133
© 2025 National Center for Youth Issues, Chattanooga, TN
All rights reserved.
Written by: Amie Dean
Published by National Center for Youth Issues
Printed in the U.S.A. • July 2025

Third party links are accurate at the time of publication, but may change over time.

The information in this book is designed to provide helpful information on the subjects discussed and is not intended to be used, nor should it be used, to diagnose or treat any mental health or medical condition. For diagnosis or treatment of any mental health or medical issue, consult a licensed counselor, psychologist, or physician. The publisher and author are not responsible for any specific mental or physical health needs that may require medical supervision, and are not liable for any damages or negative consequences from any treatment, action, application, or preparation, to any person reading or following the information in this book. References are provided for informational purposes only and do not constitute endorsement of any websites or other sources.

ASCA National Model®, Recognized ASCA Model Program® and RAMP® are registered trademarks of the American School Counselor Association. Our use of them does not imply an affiliation with or endorsement by the American School Counselor Association.

Contents

Introduction 4

    Introductory Group Session 7

Chapter 1: Understanding Conflict: Differences and Disagreements 9

Chapter 2: Conflict Resolution Styles: Understanding How We Manage Disagreements 18

Chapter 3: The Power of Words: How to Communicate Respectfully 28

Chapter 4: Active Listening: The Key to Understanding 40

Chapter 5: Nonverbal Communication: What Are You Really Saying? 48

Chapter 6: Finding Calm: Strategies for Managing Strong Emotions 59

Chapter 7: Empathy in Action: Walking in Someone Else's Shoes 69

Chapter 8: The Apology Process: Saying Sorry and Forgiving Others 79

Chapter 9: Boundaries and Balance: Finding Win-Win Solutions to Resolve Problems 90

Chapter 10: Peacekeeping in Action: Being Kind and Respectful to Solve Problems Peacefully 100

Final Group Session 111

Action Plan 112

Peaceful Conflict Resolution Group Permission Form 113

Peaceful Conflict Resolution Group Expectations 114

Group Attendance Form 115

Group Attendance Form (Example) 116

Pre- and Post-Assessment 117

Results Report 118

Results Report (Example) 119

Certificate of Completion 120

Peaceful Conflict Resolution Group Completion Letter 121

Endnotes 122

About the Author 123

About NCYI 124

Introduction

Knowing how to manage conflict will help children maintain positive, healthy relationships throughout their lives. How we deal with conflict within our relationships greatly impacts the longevity and quality of each one. The goal isn't to eliminate conflict, but to learn how to navigate difficult conversations, manage negative emotions during conflicts, and find peaceful ways to solve challenges with others. These skills take a lot of practice but will be greatly beneficial if used consistently throughout our students' lives.

This Peaceful Conflict Resolution curriculum is tailored for **2nd through 9th graders** and consists of ten thirty-minute lessons to help students learn how to solve conflict with others peacefully. The goal is to help students learn how to identify and manage emotions, listen to others and consider their perspectives, and practice kindness and respect during conflict. This curriculum recognizes the unique ways in which each student learns, emphasizing that there's no singular "correct" way to embrace these ideas. Just as each lesson is individualized to cater to diverse learning styles, the curriculum remains flexible, ensuring that every student can engage, understand, and practice these essential conflict resolution skills.

The strategic design allows students to learn new skills, connect with others, and translate their new knowledge into practice. The American School Counselor Association (ASCA®)-aligned curriculum contains an introductory lesson, ten core lessons, and a final closing lesson. Facilitators have the flexibility to include the initial and final lessons as part of the core sessions if they have extra time.

You'll find a range of essential resources in the book's concluding pages. These consist of permission and completion letters, attendance logs, a group expectation form, and a certificate of completion. You'll also find pre- and post-group surveys to measure the success of the programming and templates to share the results with interested parties. Moreover, this workbook provides a comprehensive small group action plan that will integrate effortlessly into your ASCA® evaluation document and facilitate a seamless transition from planning to assessment.

Practical and applicable, the activities provided are suitable for small and large group instruction and require no additional materials. You do not need to bring supplies beyond pencils, markers or crayons, and scratch paper; you won't need to spend hours prepping materials before meeting with your students. Everything you need is included!

See page 122 for information on Downloadable Resources.

What's Included?

Peaceful Conflict Resolution offers a comprehensive ten-lesson program and accompanying materials for facilitating group sessions. Following each detailed lesson outline, you'll find practical resources for establishing a small group within your school environment.

Mind Map: Provides an illustrated diagram of the concept or skill that can help students make connections between the concept and words they already know. Students should begin each lesson by considering the meaning of the specific conflict resolution skill. It is optional to write these, but visuals are helpful for many students. Some have found it helpful to draw the Mind Map on the board, or you can draw a tree with the concept written on the trunk and the related words on the fruit on the tree.

ASCA® Standards: Each lesson includes success criteria for the learning target.

Lesson Introduction: At the start of each lesson, we will introduce a concept and explain it to provide clarity for the upcoming story.

Circle Time Questions: This section has 3-5 optional questions for the facilitator to start the conversation. These questions allow students to deepen their understanding of the topic and build community by discussing and sharing their experiences.

Story Time: Provides stories related to the concept that should be read aloud to help students understand the concept.

Coloring Sheets: Allow younger students to visualize the concept. Students can color the sheet while the facilitator shares the initial story after the lesson is complete or take it home with them.

Discussion Questions: Students can discuss the questions posed to help them process their thoughts on personal connections with the story and concepts.

Skill Practice: Using the round-robin method, go around the table and ask students how they would practice that skill, giving each a chance to answer one question.

Additional Activities: Provides activities to help students practice and apply the concept.

Closing Considerations: Is an opportunity to review the concept and ask students to reflect on their new experience with the material.

What Would You Do – This or That?/Would You Rather: This activity allows students to consider what their course of action would be for various examples of conflict, or the skill highlighted in each chapter. The facilitator can cut out the cards and let students discuss or read aloud while moving from one side of the room to the other to communicate their choice.

Accompanying Group Documents

Action Plan: Provides the necessary information required to complete the ASCA® National Model's Classroom and Group Mindsets & Behaviors Action Plan.

Permission Form: The permission form is used to gain the permission of the student's caregivers for the child to attend the Peaceful Conflict Resolution group. Be sure to send this home about two weeks before the group starts.

Group Expectations: These provide basic expectations for the group process. The form has space for the facilitator and group to collaborate on adding additional expectations to fit their group.

Group Attendance Form: This is a blank form that allows the facilitator to track which students attended each session and what topics were discussed.

Group Attendance Form (Example): This form is an example of how to best utilize the group attendance form.

Mindsets & Behaviors Pre- and Post-Assessment: Provides an opportunity for students to share what they know of the concepts before and after they've completed the curriculum.

To measure the progress of students who participate, use the same assessment for both the pre-group and post-group assessment. Administer the pre-group assessment at the start of the instructional period, followed by instruction and practice opportunities for measured skills or knowledge.

At the end of the instructional period, administer the post-group assessment and compare the results of both assessments to identify areas of improvement and areas that need further instruction. Then calculate the average score of the pre-assessment and post-assessment and determine the percentage of improvement by subtracting the pre-assessment average from the post-assessment average and then dividing the result by the pre-assessment total. Use this pre-assessment average improvement to measure the students' progress effectively.

Percentage of Improvement Formula:
((Post-Assessment Total - Pre- Assessment Total) / Pre- Assessment Total) x 100 = Percentage of Overall Improvement

Example:
(31 Post- Assessment Total - 19 Pre- Assessment Total / 31) x 100 = 63.15% Overall Improvement

Look at your data to determine who should attend your group. Review referrals, attendance data, and achievement metrics and look for students with challenges. You can better see the impact of your small groups when strategically selecting students and closely monitoring their academic, attendance, and conduct metrics. Be sure to share the results of your intervention with your advisory council.

Results Report: The Results Report shows one way to share your data with interested parties. Remember, we want to be sure to use graphs and charts because they show our data, which has more impact than a paragraph of text. Use whatever platform you prefer to show your data, but be sure to complete the data following the group, and then share it with interested parties.

Results Report (Example): The Results Report (Example) shows what your data might resemble following the completion of the groups. You can use this form to share your data.

Peaceful Conflict Resolution Group Completion Letter: Letter written to the caregivers/guardians of students following the completion of the group. Provide students with their certificate and their group review letter during the last session.

Additional Materials: We promised to provide everything you need in this workbook, and we have. However, you will need to make copies of the pre-and post-assessments and print the Coloring Sheets. You might also print and cut the "What Would You Do - This or That?" / "Would You Rather?" games or facilitate that activity verbally. We recommend having crayons or colored pencils readily available on the table for those who wish to complete the Coloring Sheet. It might also be helpful to have some fidgets or other sensory tools accessible for your students during their group session.

We hope you find great success with your group for Peaceful Conflict Resolutions! We have included everything needed for your students to actively participate, learn, and apply the skills you teach them through these small group lessons!

Introductory Group Session

Directions & Overview

Conduct this introductory session before starting the regular lessons. This initial meeting will acclimate students to the program's structure, expectations, and foundational tools. They will learn about the Mood Meter and check-in process that will be utilized in each subsequent session.

Directions: Begin by extending a warm welcome to all participants. Communicate the group's objectives and generate enthusiasm for learning and collaboration.

Assessment: Before proceeding, read the pre-group assessment instructions aloud to the students and have each student complete the form. Carefully examine the completed forms to verify that all questions have been answered.

Introductions: Foster a sense of community by encouraging students to share their names, something about themselves, and one thing they would like to do better when they have conflict with others. Let them know they were chosen to participate based on something positive, or a specific perspective they bring to the group.

Check-In Activity: Share with students that at the start of each group session, you will do a "Vibe Check" (grades 5-9) or "Temperature Check" (grades 2-4) using the Mood Meter. The Mood Meter includes 5, 4, 3, 2, and 1 with corresponding words to describe their current mood. Each time you meet, start with a quick Question of the Day and follow with the question, "What's your number today?" Students can hold up their number quietly or answer out loud.

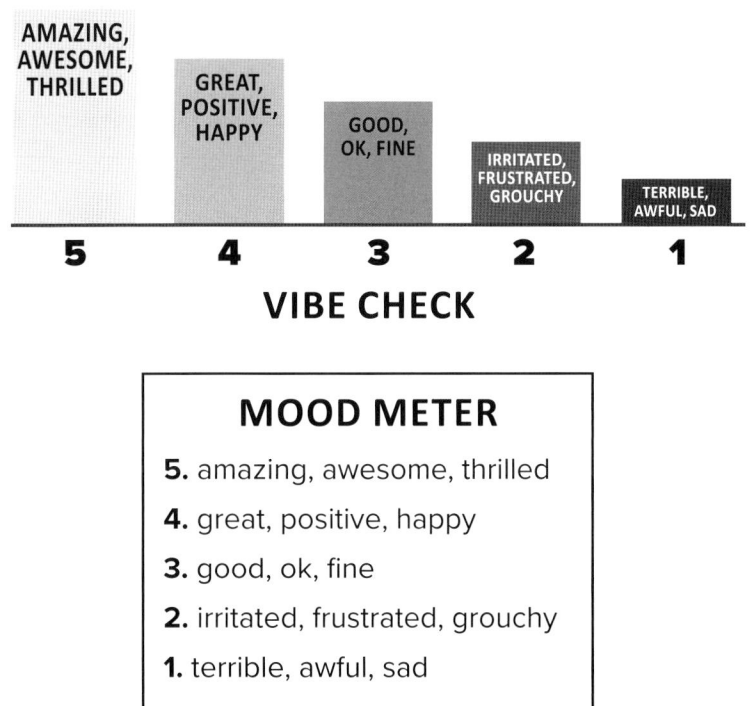

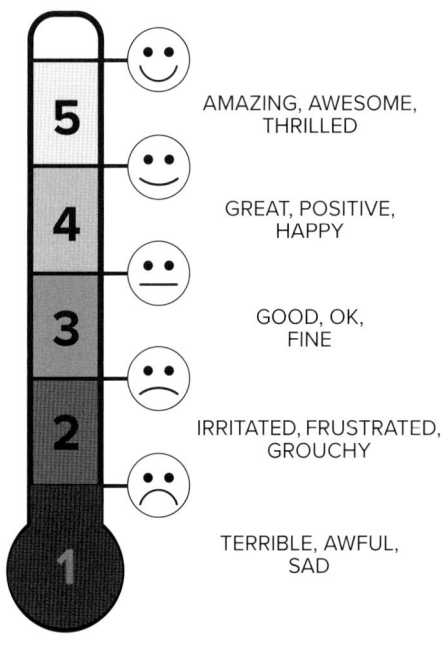

Take this initial opportunity to share with the group a few self-regulation strategies they can use when they come to group feeling like a 1 or 2. (Examples include breathing exercises, holding a laminated "Brain Break" card which excuses them from participation for 5 minutes, or for younger students, a plush animal or stress object they are allowed to hold during the lesson).

Explain the Group Format:

- Explain where and how often you will meet.

- Share the list of topics. Explain that, in each meeting, you will discuss one of the topics together, then read the Story and answer questions.

- Discuss the logistics of what they'll do while you are reading; they'll be eating (if it is a lunch group) or completing their Coloring Sheet.

- Explain that they'll have time to work in pairs for the Skill Practice portion and play a "What Would You Do - This or That?" / "Would You Rather?" game.

- Finally, explain that at the end of each session, they'll be asked to give a one-sentence overview of what they've learned and how they plan to practice that lesson topic throughout the week.

Review Group Expectations: Print a copy of the Group Expectations. Review the expectations together with the students and answer questions as they arise. Collaborate with your group to determine whether you need to modify or add expectations.

Group Conclusion: Ask each student to summarize the information they learned from this session into one sentence. Students may share with their partners or the group.

Note to Facilitators: You can customize the material to fit the needs of your group. If your students are not yet readers, you can read the "What Would You Do - This or That?" / "Would You Rather?" activity questions aloud and request that students move to different sides of the room to show their answers. If you're working with more reserved students, they can write their responses to questions instead of sharing them aloud or break into smaller teams to discuss. Some facilitators may incorporate traditional games into the lessons if they have longer session times. Remember, the workbook is just the framework, but you will bring it to life!

Understanding Conflict: Differences and Disagreements

MIND MAP

Conflict — A struggle or problem between opposing forces, people, or ideas; dispute

On the board, draw a Mind Map and ask students to consider the meaning of **Conflict**.

- **Argument** – when people talk loudly or get upset because they don't agree with each other
- **Disagreement** – when people have different ideas or opinions about something
- **Fight** – When people argue, and it gets physical like pushing or hitting; when conflict becomes unsafe
- **Misunderstanding** – when someone gets the wrong idea, which can cause confusion or upset
- **Miscommunication** – when people don't understand each other correctly because the words or messages are unclear
- **Personal issue** – When people don't get along because of differences in personality or past events

ASCA® STANDARDS

- **B-LS 4.** Self-motivation and self-direction for learning
- **B-SS 2.** Positive, respectful, and supportive relationships

DIRECTIONS

- Review the Group Expectations.
- Conduct a student check-in with the Mood Meter.
- Review and discuss the Mind Map.
- Read the Lesson Introduction and ask the Circle Time Questions.
- Read the Story and follow with Discussion Questions.
- Complete the Skill Practice, What Would You Do – This or That, and Additional Activities as time allows.
- Wrap up with the Closing Considerations for each lesson.

In a small group format, conduct your student check-in using the Mood Meter. Ask students to hold up their number (5, 4, 3, 2, or 1) to show the type of day they are having. Validate each student's number and thank them for sharing. If time, you may ask volunteers to elaborate with one reason they chose their number. Ask the group if they have anything to say to be helpful and encouraging to other group members who shared a 1 or 2 for their check-in. Model kind and uplifting responses for the group each week so they can learn how to respond when a group member is having a tough day.

TEMPERATURE CHECK

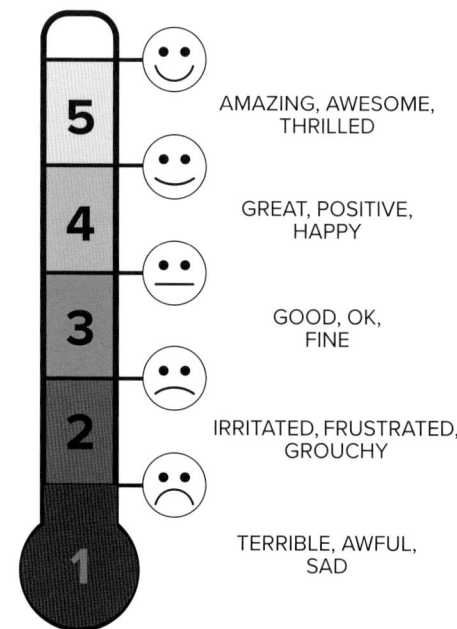

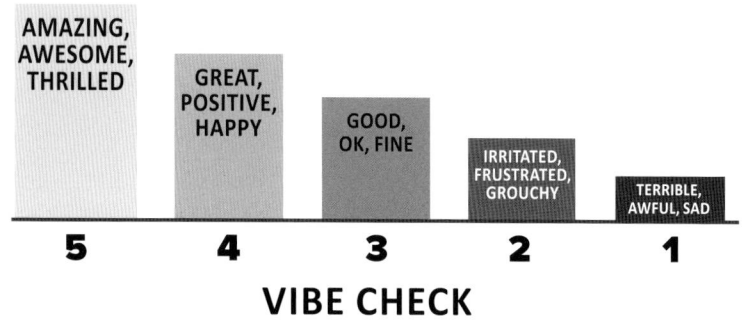

VIBE CHECK

30-MINUTE GROUPS: **PEACEFUL CONFLICT RESOLUTION**

Review the Group Expectations before reviewing the Mind Map. Then, read the Lesson Introduction and ask the Circle Time Questions before reading the Story and the Discussion Questions. Students can work in pairs to craft their responses or share with the whole group. Complete the Skill Practice, What Would You Do - This or That, and Additional Activities as time allows. Be sure to complete the Closing Considerations with each lesson.

LESSON INTRODUCTION

Have you ever felt mad at someone you love? Have you felt frustrated with someone you are friends with or even someone you don't know at all? Raise your hand if you have ever had an argument with a brother, sister, friend, or classmate. Notice that all of us said yes to at least one of these examples. That is because having conflict with other people is a part of our human experience. It is unavoidable. The good news is that conflict is manageable, and we can all learn ways to navigate it successfully. Learning how to deal with conflict in many types of situations and different relationships is one of the most important skills any of us will ever learn. Facing conflicts and resolving them peacefully will help us maintain healthy relationships where we feel respected, happy, and safe.

Three types of conflict for today's focus:

- **Misunderstanding:** When we don't understand what someone meant or said, leading to confusion or hurt feelings.
- **Disagreement:** When two people have different opinions or ideas.
- **Personal Issue:** When we don't get along with someone because of differences in personality or past events.

CIRCLE TIME QUESTIONS

Ask students to reflect and share their answers to the following questions with the group. Larger groups may need to be broken into smaller groups to give students ample time to share their answers and deepen the conversation.

- What is the difference between a misunderstanding and a disagreement?
- Can you think of a time you had a misunderstanding with a friend or family member?
- Share a time when you had a personal issue with someone.

STORY TIME

Hand out the Coloring Sheets and crayons or markers to younger students while the facilitator reads the story, if desired.

The Class Project

It was a regular morning in science when Ms. Ferrell assigned a group project about sea turtles. Two friends, Adriana and Liam, were assigned as partners, and they got together to discuss their topic. But quickly, their excitement turned into frustration.

Adriana suggested they focus on the sea turtle's life cycle. "It's so cool how they grow from eggs to adults!" she said excitedly.

But Liam disagreed. "I think we should talk about how pollution affects sea turtles. That's what's really hurting them."

Adriana frowned. "I think the life cycle is more interesting. We could do a whole section on how they grow!"

Liam crossed his arms. "But pollution is a bigger problem! If we don't focus on that, we're missing the point."

The conversation quickly escalated. "You're not listening to any of my ideas!" Liam fumed.

"I am! You're just not listening to me!" Adriana huffed back.

Both were feeling very annoyed, and the project felt like it was falling apart.

Ms. Ferrell came over to their table and asked what was going on. After hearing their argument, she said, "It seems like you both care a lot about the project. Why don't you take a moment to listen to each other's thoughts without talking about your own? You might find a way to make both of your ideas work."

Adriana and Liam sat in silence for a moment, then Adriana spoke first. "I guess I could see how pollution is a big issue for sea turtles. I wonder if we can find a way to talk about their life cycle, too."

Liam nodded. "I think we can. We could talk about both—how pollution affects them and how they grow. That way, we both get to share what's important to us."

They smiled at each other. "Let's divide the work," Adriana suggested. "I'll research the life cycle, and you can focus on pollution."

The two friends worked together, combining their ideas into a great presentation. Ms. Ferrell praised them for working through their disagreement and finding a solution.

Adriana and Liam learned that talking through a problem and listening to each other is a great way to solve a conflict.

DISCUSSION QUESTIONS

- Did the students in the story have a misunderstanding or a disagreement?
- What do you think caused the conflict?

- What mistakes do you think they made in the beginning?
- What would you have done if a classmate wouldn't listen to your ideas?
- How did they solve their conflict?

SKILL PRACTICE

Using the round-robin method, go around the table and ask students to identify which of the three types of conflict is evident in each scenario, giving everyone a chance to answer one question. You can adapt this Skill Practice to allow students to respond in pairs or write their answers on paper.

SCENARIO 1:

Mikayla asked her friend Jasmine if she wanted to hang out after school, and Jasmine said, "I can't today, I have to finish my homework." Mikayla thought Jasmine was upset with her and didn't want to spend time with her. The next day, Mikayla felt hurt and didn't speak to Jasmine. Later, Jasmine explained that she just needed to finish homework and was still happy to spend time with Mikayla. This is an example of a _____. **Answer:** Misunderstanding

SCENARIO 2:

In class, Jack and Malik argued about what game to play during recess. Jack wanted to play basketball, but Malik wanted to play kickball. They argued about it for a while but then decided to play kickball first and then basketball afterward. This is an example of a _____. **Answer:** Disagreement

SCENARIO 3:

Hector and Noah had been close friends for a long time, but lately, Hector noticed that Noah was acting distant and ignoring him at lunch. Hector tried talking to Noah, but Noah didn't want to talk about what was going on. They decided to take a break from talking for a while to give each other space. This is an example of a _____. **Answer:** Personal Issue

SCENARIO 4:

Ryan and Sarah were choosing what movie to watch. Ryan wanted to watch an action movie, while Sarah wanted to watch a scary movie. They disagreed, but after talking it through, they decided to pick a movie that had both action and scary moments so they could both enjoy it. This is an example of a _____. **Answer:** Disagreement

SCENARIO 5:

Jacob and Olivia were riding the bus to school together, and Jacob said, "I like those red boots!" Olivia thought he was making fun of her new boots, so she got upset. Jacob meant that he thought they looked cool, but Olivia didn't understand and felt embarrassed. After talking, Olivia realized it was actually a compliment. This is an example of a _____. **Answer:** Misunderstanding

SCENARIO 6:

Martin and Hudson used to play soccer together every day, but recently, Martin noticed that Hudson had been making fun of him in front of others. Martin felt hurt, but he didn't know why Hudson was doing it. When Martin finally asked Hudson about it, Hudson admitted he had been feeling jealous. They had a serious talk about how they could be better friends and solve the problem that was affecting their friendship. This is an example of a _____. **Answer:** Personal Issue

ADDITIONAL ACTIVITIES

OPTION 1: PERSONAL PLEDGE

Ask students to write a personal pledge that includes three commitments to how they will try to handle conflict at school, home, or with friends.

OPTION 2: PICTURE BOOKS

Read a picture book (2nd-4th) such as *Enemy Pie* by Derek Munson, *A Big Guy Took My Ball!* By Mo Willems, or *The Line in the Sand* by Thao Lam. Ask students to answer a few questions: Why did the characters have conflict? How did they solve it?

OPTION 3: CONFLICT TREE WORKSHEET

Using the **Conflict Tree worksheet**, write a specific conflict on the trunk and ask students which type of conflict it represents. Ask students to brainstorm causes and label the branches with the causes students offer. Begin by doing this activity as a group, then invite the students to do it individually or in pairs. Ask them to label a conflict they have experienced personally on the trunk of their tree. Then students will label the branches with the causes of the conflict. Finally, ask students to choose what type of conflict it was based on the six types of conflict highlighted on the Mind Map.

CLOSING CONSIDERATIONS

Conflict is a part of our everyday life. It is unavoidable, but the good news is we get to choose how we resolve it. We will have misunderstandings, disagreements, and sometimes personal differences in all kinds of relationships. Understanding what conflict is and what causes it can help us figure out how to resolve it. In our future sessions, we will learn more about how to respond to conflicts. We will learn how to show self-awareness, choose our words carefully, and work with others to find peaceful resolutions.

Ask students to summarize the content of this session's lesson in one sentence.

Conflict Tree

Label a conflict you have experienced personally on the trunk of your tree.
Next, write the reasons, or causes, that led to the conflict in the boxes on the branches.

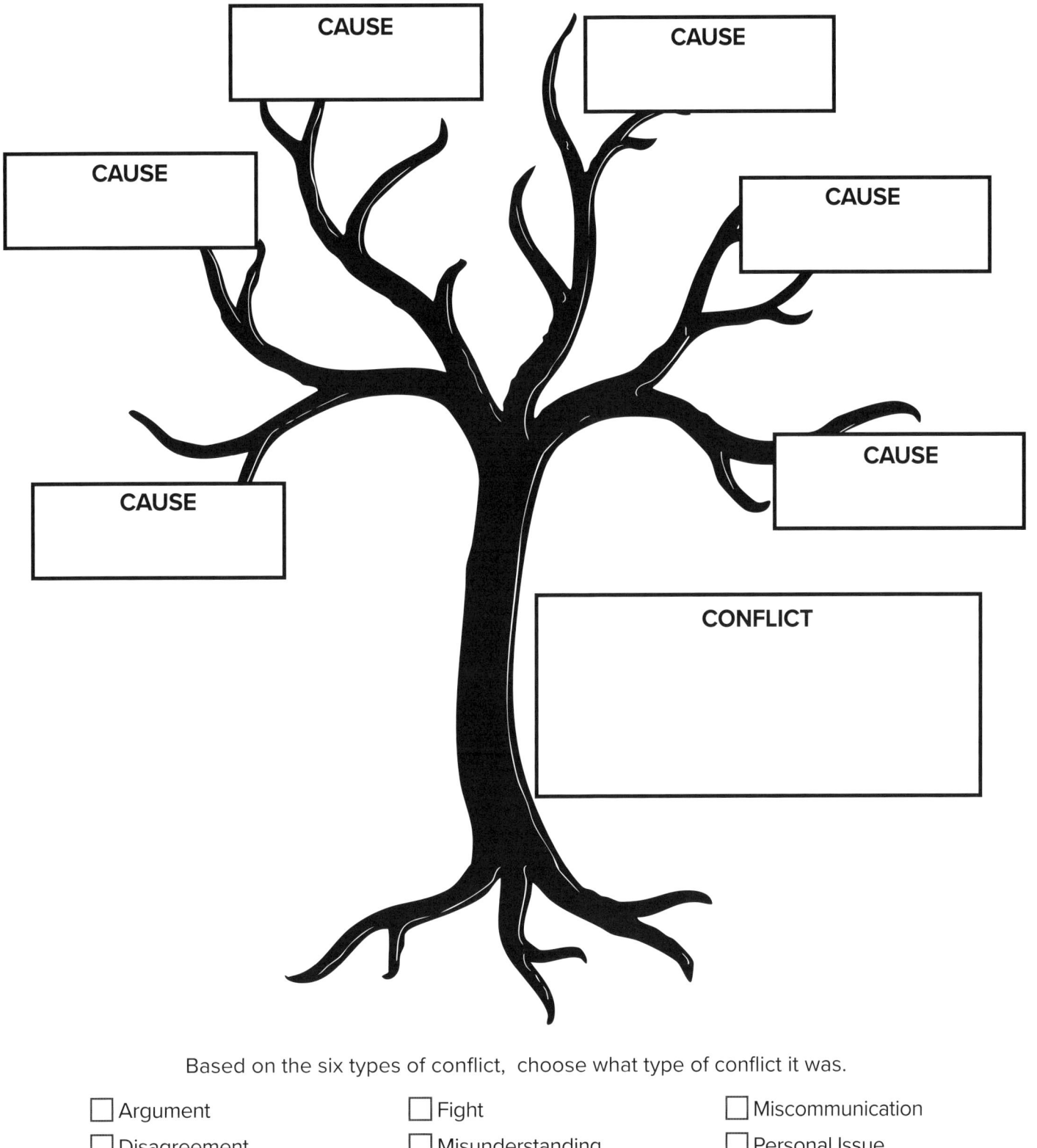

Based on the six types of conflict, choose what type of conflict it was.

☐ Argument　　　　　　☐ Fight　　　　　　　　☐ Miscommunication
☐ Disagreement　　　　☐ Misunderstanding　　☐ Personal Issue

30-MINUTE GROUPS: PEACEFUL CONFLICT RESOLUTION

"WHAT WOULD YOU DO - THIS OR THAT?" GAME

Playing the What Would You Do - This or That? Game is a fun and engaging activity for students to develop their critical thinking skills. Students will reflect on their experience, evaluate their options based on their preferences, and reflect on the opinions of others, providing a different perspective and strengthening their sense of connection to one another.

What Would You Do–This or That?

Copy and cut out the questions for small groups to discuss, or have each person stand in the center of the room and move towards one side or the other to show their vote for either option as the facilitator reads the questions aloud.

What would you do if a friend made fun of you in front of others?
- Make fun of them, too
- Wait and talk about it with your friend later

What would you do if you and your brother couldn't decide who gets to sit in the front seat?
- Argue until you get your way
- Play rock, paper, scissors and winner gets the front seat

What would you do if your pencil box went missing during lunch?
- Accuse several people of stealing it
- Talk to your teacher to get help

What would you do if a student on your bus makes fun of you, and you feel embarrassed?
- Stand up and argue
- Ask the bus driver if you can move seats

What would you do if your parent said you would go to the park, but now they are not able to take you?
- Tell them you understand sometimes plans change.
- Start crying and yelling, "that's not fair"

What would you do if you and another student wanted the same paint to use in art class, and there is only one?
- Tell the other student you will not be friends if they don't give it to you.
- Ask to move your seat to their table so you can share

30-MINUTE GROUPS: PEACEFUL CONFLICT RESOLUTION

Conflict Resolution Styles: Understanding How We Manage Disagreements

MIND MAP

Conflict Resolution – Finding a way to solve a problem or disagreement between people in a peaceful and fair way

On the board, draw a Mind Map and ask students to consider the meaning of **Conflict Resolution**.

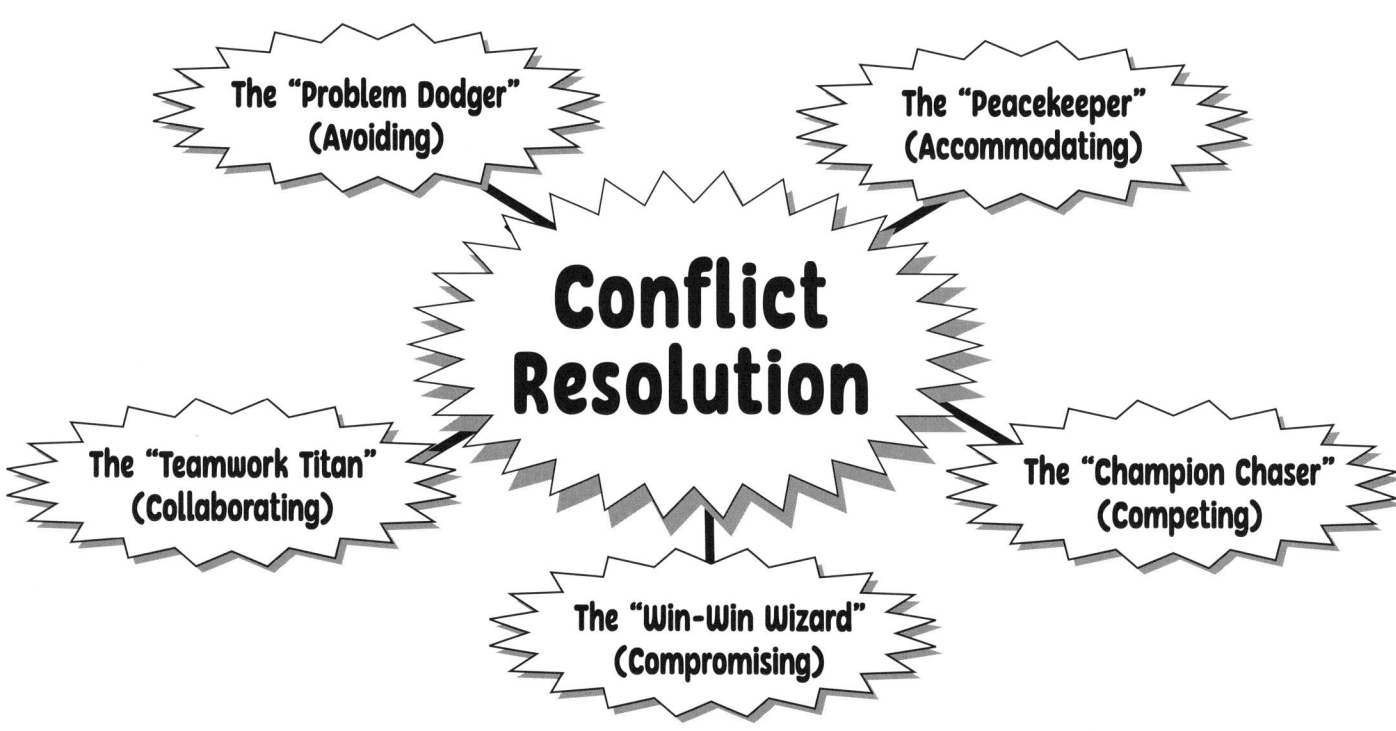

5 Styles of Conflict Resolution: (based on Thomas-Kilmann Model)[1]

 **The "Problem Dodger" (Avoiding):** Someone who tries to ignore the problem and hopes it goes away on its own.

 **The "Peacekeeper" (Accommodating):** When someone gives in to what the other person wants, just to keep things calm and happy.

 The "Champion Chaser" (Competing): A person who tries really hard to win the argument or situation, no matter what, even if it means the other person loses.

 **The "Win-Win Wizard" (Compromising):** A person who is good at getting everyone involved to give up something or meet halfway and find a solution that works for all.

 **The "Teamwork Titan" (Collaborating):** This is when someone is good at working with others as a team to find a solution that makes everyone feel satisfied or happy.

ASCA® STANDARDS

- **B-LS 4.** Self-Motivation and self-direction for learning
- **B-SMS 2.** Self-discipline and self-control
- **B-SMS 7.** Demonstrates effective coping skills
- **B-SS 2.** Positive, respectful supportive relationships with students
- **B-SS 6.** Effective collaboration and cooperation skills

DIRECTIONS

- Review the Group Expectations.
- Conduct a student check-in with the Mood Meter.
- Review and discuss the Mind Map.
- Read the Lesson Introduction and ask the Circle Time Questions.
- Read the Story and follow with Discussion Questions.
- Complete the Skill Practice, What Would You Do – This or That, and Additional Activities as time allows.
- Wrap up with the Closing Considerations for each lesson.

In a small group format, conduct your student check-in using the Mood Meter. Ask students to hold up their number (5, 4, 3, 2, or 1) to show the type of day they are having. Validate each student's number and thank them for sharing. If time, you may ask volunteers to elaborate with one reason they chose their number. Ask the group if they have anything to say to be helpful and encouraging to other group members who shared a 1 or 2 for their check-in. Model kind and uplifting responses for the group each week so they can learn how to respond when a group member is having a tough day.

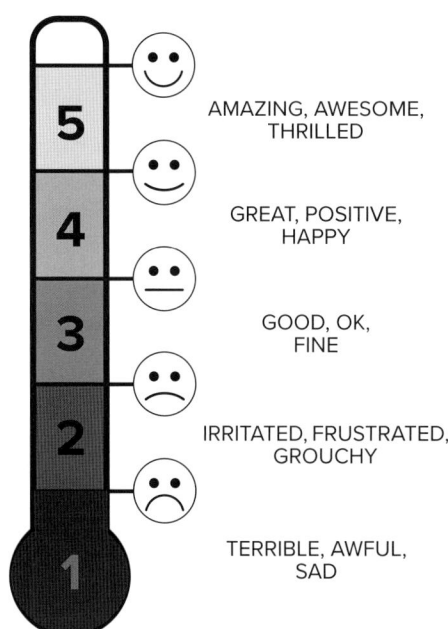

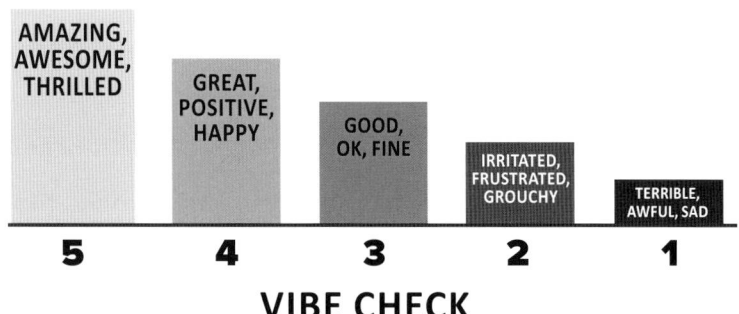

Review the Group Expectations before reviewing the Mind Map. Then, read the Lesson Introduction and ask the Circle Time Questions before reading the Story and the Discussion Questions. Students can work in pairs to craft their responses or share with the whole group. Complete the Skill Practice, What Would You Do - This or That, and Additional Activities as time allows. Be sure to complete the Closing Considerations with each lesson.

LESSON INTRODUCTION

Last time we met, we talked about the different kinds of conflict we might have with others. Who can name one of the types we discussed? (disagreement, misunderstanding, argument, etc.) Try to think of a time you've had conflict with someone. Please share how you managed the problem or describe the outcome. (Allow several minutes for partner/group discussion.)

How we manage or resolve a disagreement or problem with someone is called **conflict resolution**. It's a way of finding peaceful solutions when you don't agree. Conflict is normal, and everyone will experience it. What's most important is how we manage and solve those disagreements!

Using our Mind Map, we'll learn more about five different conflict resolution styles. Some people might try to avoid the conflict, others just want to win, and some people try to work together to find a solution that works for everyone. By understanding these styles, and identifying your own style, you'll learn multiple ways to resolve disagreements calmly and respectfully.

CIRCLE TIME QUESTIONS

After the Mind Map discussion, ask students to reflect and share their answers to the following questions with the group. Larger groups may need to be broken into smaller groups to give students ample time to share their answers and deepen the conversation.

- What does it mean to be a "Champion Chaser?" What makes this style challenging?
- Do you think it's possible for one person to use different styles at different times?
- Which one of the five styles best describes how you personally manage conflict?
- Which style do you believe allows mutual respect and success for all people involved?
- Identify a style you would like to try to use more often.

STORY TIME

Hand out the Coloring Sheets and crayons or markers to younger students while the facilitator reads the story, if desired.

Race at Recess

It was recess time for Ms. Lee's 5th grade class at Sweet Apple Elementary. The students were running, playing, and having fun. Four friends—Maya, Jose, Bella, and Jayden—decided to play a game of tag.

At first, everything was going well. Maya tagged Jose, and then he chased after Jayden and everyone was playing together. It wasn't too long before the group realized that Maya was the slowest, so everyone only chased her as soon as they were tagged. Maya knew she wasn't the fastest runner, but she took dance classes with Bella, so she thought Bella would at least give her a break!

Maya suddenly slowed down and walked off to the side while watching the others run. "I think I'll just sit out for now," she said quietly. Her friends didn't notice at first, but after a moment, Jose stopped running and looked over at her.

"Hey, Maya! Why are you sitting over there?" he asked, trying to catch his breath.

Maya shrugged while keeping her eyes on the ground. "I'm just tired. I don't want to run anymore."

Jose frowned, but he didn't say anything. He went back to running, but a lot faster this time. He liked the idea of winning and didn't want to lose any opportunity to catch someone. He chased down Jayden, tagged him, and yelled, "I win again! Who's up for a race?"

Jayden grinned. "I'm ready! Let's race across the whole playground. Whoever wins gets to be 'it' next."

Jose immediately perked up. "I'm definitely faster than you," he said, his voice full of confidence. "I'll win for sure!"

While the boys got ready to race, Bella noticed Maya still sitting on the bench, looking bored. She knew that Maya didn't really want to quit the game, so she tried to figure out a way to get her back with the group. She ran to Jose and Jayden, who were already getting ready for the race.

"Hey, what if we do something different?" Bella suggested. "Instead of just racing, maybe we could add some fun challenges in the game—like dancing or doing silly moves when you're tagged. That way, Maya can play with us, too."

Jose, still focused on winning, gave her the side eye. "That sounds kind of lame. I just want to race and be 'it' next." Jayden shook his head in agreement.

Bella said, "I know, but that keeps Maya from playing. If we try this for a little while, we'll all get to play and do something we like. We can still race if you want, but let's make it more fun for everybody."

Jose thought about it for a moment, then shook his head. "Well, I'm still going to win," he said, running off again without waiting for anyone to respond. He sped up quickly, eager to prove he was the fastest.

Bella went over to Maya, who was still sitting on the bench. "You can join us whenever you want, Maya. We're going to make it fun, I promise."

Maya hesitated but then stood up with a smile. "Okay, I'll try it. I want to play again."

As the group continued, the game got better and better. Everyone was laughing, doing funny moves when tagged, and cheering each other on. Maya impressed the others with some of her amazing dance moves. Even Jose, who still wanted to win, started enjoying the silly challenges – well, some of them! The game ended up being fun for everyone, and Maya felt happy to be included.

DISCUSSION QUESTIONS

- Share an example from the story of the "Win-Win Wizard" style of problem solving.
- When Maya walked off quietly to sit out, what style of conflict resolution did she represent?
- Which character best represents the "Champion Chaser" style?
- Which character do you feel is most like you? Why?
- Who do you think represented the most peaceful approach to the conflict in the story? Why?

SKILL PRACTICE

Using the round-robin method, go around the table and ask students how they would practice each skill, giving everyone a chance to answer one question. You can adapt this Skill Practice to allow students to respond in pairs or write their answers on paper.

1. How would you practice being a Peacekeeper (Accommodating) if:

    - There are three kids in your family but only two ice-cream treats left?
    - You and one of your classmates both want to be Line Leader for the week?
    - One of your friends is being left out of a party because they don't have social media?

2. How could you be a Teamwork Titan (Collaborating) when:

    - The teacher is allowing the class to listen to music, and six different suggestions have been made?
    - Your soccer team is going to eat after a big win and no one can agree on which restaurant to go to?

Allow students to choose one of the five conflict resolution styles and share an example of when and how they can apply it.

ADDITIONAL ACTIVITIES

Here are sample scenarios that can be used in the various activities below:

- Two friends argue over who gets the last cookie.
- One student wants to join a game, but the others don't want them to.
- A student wants to play basketball but doesn't have a ball.

OPTION 1: GROUPS ACT OUT RESOLUTION STYLES

Divide students into pairs or small groups. Give each group a scenario where there is conflict. Assign each group a different conflict resolution style (Avoiding, Accommodating, Competing, Compromising, or Collaborating). Have each group act out the scenario using the assigned style. Examples:

- **Avoiding:** One person walks away or ignores the problem.
- **Accommodating:** One person gives in to the other person's wishes.
- **Competing:** One person always wants to be right and gets upset if they don't win.
- **Compromising:** Both people agree to take turns.
- **Collaborating:** All people in the group work together to come up with a fair solution where everyone can play with the ball for equal amounts of time.

OPTION 2: INDIVIDUALS ACT OUT RESOLUTION STYLES

Write down the five conflict resolution styles on separate pieces of paper and put them in a container or on a wheel at www.wheelofnames.com. Each student takes turns drawing a piece of paper and acting out that conflict resolution style without speaking. The rest of the class tries to guess which style they're acting out. Discuss how that style could be used in real-life situations.

OPTION 3: CONFLICT RESOLUTION COMIC STRIPS

- Provide students with the **Conflict Resolution Comic Strips** templates and ask them to create a short comic illustrating a conflict between two characters (see below). They should show the conflict and the resolution using one of the five conflict resolution styles. Once the students finish, they can share their comics with the class and explain how the style they chose helped solve the problem.

CLOSING CONSIDERATIONS

Today, we learned about five ways to solve problems with others:

- **Avoiding** – walking away from the problem
- **Accommodating** – letting the other person have their way
- **Competing** – trying to win
- **Compromising** – both people give a little to agree
- **Collaborating** – working together to find the best answer

There is more than one right way to solve a problem. It depends on what's going on and who is with you.

When you have a disagreement, remember to stay calm, listen to others, and try to work together. Think about the five ways to solve problems and pick the one that helps everyone feel safe and respected.

Ask students to summarize the content of this session's lesson in one sentence.

Conflict Resolution Comic Strips

Create your own comic strip showing the conflict in the box on the left and a resolution in the box on the right using one of these resolutions styles: Avoiding, Accommodating, Competing, Compromising, or Collaborating. List which style is used below each.

Conflict

Resolution

Conflict Resolution Style:_____

Conflict

Resolution

Conflict Resolution Style:_____

Conflict

Resolution

Conflict Resolution Style:_____

"WHAT WOULD YOU DO - THIS OR THAT?" GAME

Playing the What Would You Do - This or That? Game is a fun and engaging activity for students to develop their critical thinking skills. Students will reflect on their experience, evaluate their options based on their preferences, and reflect on the opinions of others, providing a different perspective and strengthening their sense of connection to one another.

What Would You Do–This or That?

Copy and cut out the questions for small groups to discuss, or have each person stand in the center of the room and move towards one side or the other to show their vote for either option as the facilitator reads the questions aloud.

What would you do if you disagree with a friend?
- Find a solution together (Collaborating)
- Let them have their way (Accommodating)

What would you do if you didn't want to deal with a conflict?
- Walk away (Avoiding)
- Try to win the argument (Competing)

What would you do if everyone had a different idea in a group?
- Try to let everyone have a say (Compromising)
- Stick to your idea (Competing)

What would you do if there's a disagreement in a group project?
- Work together to solve it (Collaborating)
- Let someone else decide (Accommodating)

What would you do if someone cuts in line?
- Confront them (Competing)
- Let it go (Avoiding)

What would you do if your friend wanted the same seat as you?
- Discuss and find a solution (Collaborating)
- Let them sit there (Accommodating)

30-MINUTE GROUPS: **PEACEFUL CONFLICT RESOLUTION**

THE POWER OF WORDS: HOW TO COMMUNICATE RESPECTFULLY

MIND MAP

Respectful Communication – the practice of communicating with others in a way that shows consideration, appreciation, and understanding.

On the board, draw a Mind Map and ask students to consider the meaning of **Respectful Communication**.

- SELF-AWARENESS
- WORD CHOICE
- REFLECTION
- LISTENING
- PATIENCE
- UNDERSTANDING

RESPECTUL COMMUNICATION

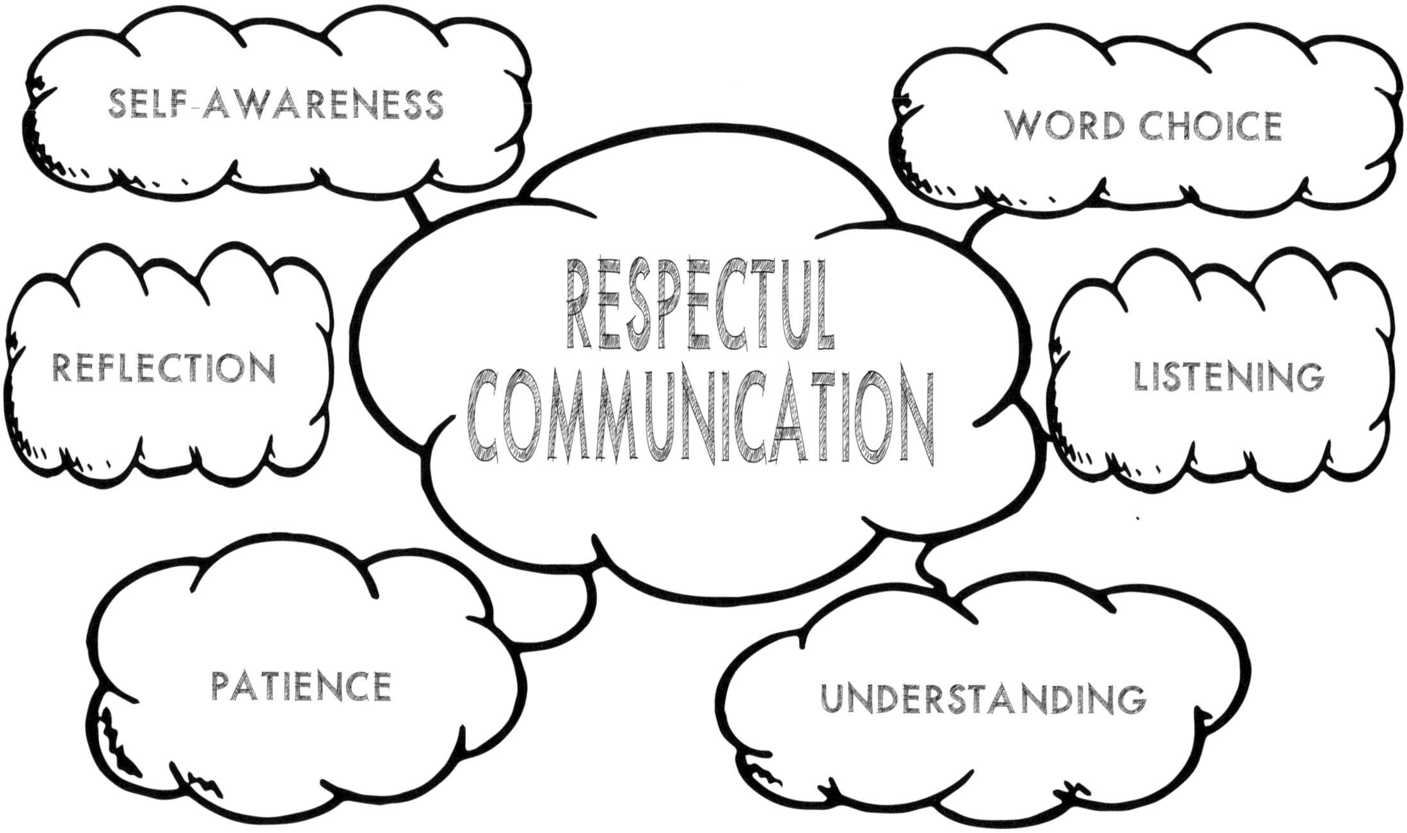

- **Self-Awareness** – the ability to understand your own feelings, thoughts, and actions and how it affects your choices and behavior
- **Word Choice** – choosing words that are considerate, honest, and helpful to the situation
- **Listening** – paying attention to what someone else is saying without interrupting
- **Patience** – staying calm while waiting for your turn even if you don't like what you hear
- **Reflection** – thinking about how your words or actions have impacted a person or situation
- **Understanding** – caring about how others feel and showing them that their thoughts and feelings matter

ASCA® STANDARDS

- **B-SMS 2.** Self-discipline and self-control
- **B-SS 1**. Effective oral communication skills
- **B-SS 2.** Positive, respectful relationships with students
- **B-SS 6**. Effective collaboration and cooperation skills
- **B-SS 9.** Social maturity and behaviors appropriate to the situation

DIRECTIONS

- Review the Group Expectations.
- Conduct a student check-in with the Mood Meter.
- Review and discuss the Mind Map.
- Read the Lesson Introduction and ask the Circle Time Questions.
- Read the Story and follow with Discussion Questions.
- Complete the Skill Practice, What Would You Do – This or That, and Additional Activities as time allows.
- Wrap up with the Closing Considerations for each lesson.

In a small group format, conduct your student check-in using the Mood Meter. Ask students to hold up their number (5, 4, 3, 2, or 1) to show the type of day they are having. Validate each student's number and thank them for sharing. If time, you may ask volunteers to elaborate with one reason they chose their number. Ask the group if they have anything to say to be helpful and encouraging to other group members who shared a 1 or 2 for their check-in. Model kind and uplifting responses for the group each week so they can learn how to respond when a group member is having a tough day.

TEMPERATURE CHECK

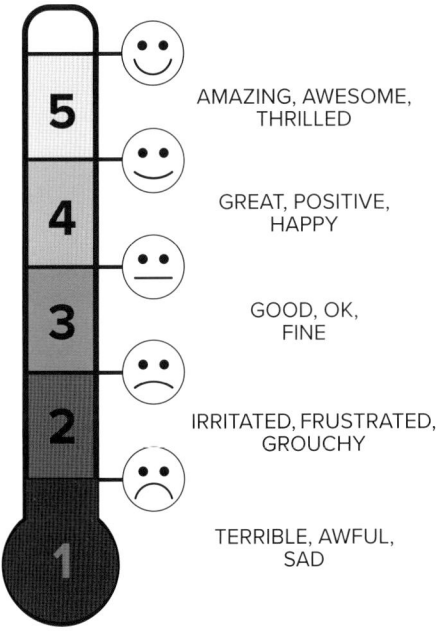

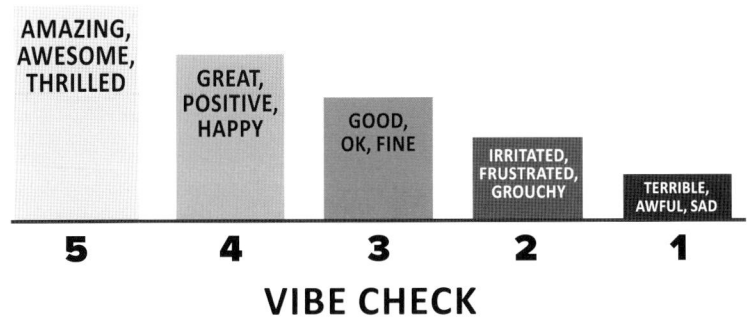

VIBE CHECK

Review the Group Expectations before reviewing the Mind Map. Then, read the Lesson Introduction and ask the Circle Time Questions before reading the Story and the Discussion Questions. Students can work in pairs to craft their responses or share with the whole group. Complete the Skill Practice, What Would You Do - This or That, and Additional Activities as time allows. Be sure to complete the Closing Considerations with each lesson.

LESSON INTRODUCTION

Have you ever said something, or texted/posted something, that you wished you could take back? Words have the power to build or break relationships. It is important to choose our words carefully so we can create and maintain positive relationships with friends, family, teachers, and peers. It involves actively listening, choosing your words carefully, and valuing others' perspectives, even if they are different from yours. Respectful communication helps us express our thoughts, feelings, and opinions in a way that doesn't hurt others, while also allowing them to share their own.

An easy way to remember this is by following the 3 R's of respectful communication:

- **Receive** – Listen carefully and try to understand; avoid distractions or interruptions.
- **Repeat** – Repeat what you think you heard the other person say.
- **Respond** – Offer a respectful comment or question or make a helpful suggestion.

CIRCLE TIME QUESTIONS

Ask students to reflect and share their answers to the following questions with the group. Larger groups may need to be broken into smaller groups to give students ample time to share their answers and deepen the conversation.

- Can you think of a time when someone said something to you that you thought was disrespectful? Why did you find it disrespectful?
- Why do you think we often lose patience during conflict? Why is it hard to stay calm?
- What can you do to help yourself choose respectful words when you feel angry or frustrated?
- Can you finish this well-known saying? If you don't have anything nice to say... (don't say anything at all.) Can you think of a time when this would be a good rule to follow?

STORY TIME

Hand out the Coloring Sheets and crayons or markers to younger students while the facilitator reads the story, if desired.

A Friendship Tested

It was finally the weekend, and Deja and Jessie walked to the local park to hang out with a group of friends. The weather was great, and everyone was in a good mood—until Deja and Jessie had the first argument of their friendship.

The two had been friends for a long time, but recently after moving up to a new school, things had started to feel different. Deja was quieter than usual, and Jessie had been more focused on hanging out with other friends, leaving Deja feeling left out a lot lately. They had always been able to talk through problems in the past, but this time, it felt like they just couldn't communicate.

"Hey, Deja, are you coming with us over to the skate park?" Jessie asked, her voice casual but impatient. Earlier that morning, she had been excited to meet up with friends, but now Deja wasn't sure if she wanted to stay. She noticed how much fun Jessie was having with her new friends and how often Jessie did stuff with them without even asking if Deja wanted to join. She had tried to ignore it, but today, it finally felt like too much.

"I don't know, Jessie," Deja replied, her voice annoyed. "You've been talking it up with everyone but me this whole time, and I've just been sitting here alone. You never even ask if I want to hang out anymore. It's like you don't even care."

Jessie glared, surprised by the anger in Deja's voice. "What are you talking about? I've been busy, that's all. I didn't know you were upset. You could have also talked to everyone or said something earlier instead of sitting there all dark and moody. "

Deja shook her head. "I'm trying to tell you how I feel, but it seems like every time I talk to you lately, you get mad or bark at me."

Jessie was really getting annoyed. "That's not fair, Deja! You know we have always been best friends, right? I don't know what you want me to do. You're always so sensitive about everything. Why can't you just relax "

Deja's chest felt heavy. She didn't want to argue, but it felt like Jessie was dismissing her feelings and not listening to her. "Maybe I don't always want to hang out with everyone else, Jessie. But I do want to feel like I matter to you. When you raise your voice at me, it doesn't feel like we are best friends."

Jessie opened her mouth to respond, but she stopped before she said something she couldn't take back. Both girls sat in frustrated silence, and it got uncomfortable. The tension between them felt like a wall they couldn't break down. One of their other friends, Michele, who had not left for the skate park yet, stood up and walked over to them.

"Hey, guys, I don't mean to interrupt, but I overheard what was said, and I think you both need to hear something," Michele said while looking at both of them with concern. "Deja, I can see you're hurt. And Jessie, I know you didn't mean to upset her. But you're both using words that are making this worse."

Deja wiped her eyes and sighed. "I know. I just... I feel like Jessie doesn't care anymore, and it hurts."

Michele nodded. "I get it, Deja. But Jessie can't know how you feel if you don't tell her. And Jessie, you can't just brush it off when she's upset. You need to listen to her and maybe try to ask questions without raising your voice. Don't just assume she's overreacting."

Jessie looked down, feeling ashamed. "I didn't mean to make you feel like that, Deja. I guess I've been so caught up in everything else that I didn't notice how you were feeling. But I do care. I'm sorry."

Deja took a deep breath. "I don't need you to be perfect, Jessie. I just want you to notice if I'm upset and not talk to me in such an angry way. You're my best friend, and I need you to listen and speak more calmly."

Jessie nodded. "I understand now. I'll do better, I promise. I don't want you to feel like I don't care, and I was wrong to talk to you that way."

Michele smiled and gave them both a high-five. "See? A little honesty and respect go a long way."

As Deja and Jessie started walking toward the skate park, they both smiled. Each of them knew that staying friends as they got older wouldn't always be easy, but that their friendship was worth it.

DISCUSSION QUESTIONS

- How did Deja's feelings of being left out impact her communication with Jessie?
- Why did Jessie react the way she did when Deja said she felt left out?
- What word choices could Jessie have avoided in the beginning to help the situation?
- How did Michele help Deja and Jessie understand the importance of respectful communication?
- Can you find examples in the story of respectful communication such as good listening, patience, self-awareness, and understanding?

SKILL PRACTICE

Using the round-robin method, go around the table and ask students how they would practice each skill, giving everyone a chance to answer one question. You can adapt this Skill Practice to allow students to respond in pairs or write their answers on paper.

Share this list of scenarios that involve conflict or difficult conversations:

- A friend borrowed something without asking and didn't return it.
- A classmate made a hurtful comment about your clothes.
- You overheard your brother telling a friend a secret you told him not to share.

Have each student pick a scenario and then, in pairs, practice respectful communication to respond to the situation. The challenge is to **choose words** that are respectful, honest, and considerate of the other person's feelings. Challenge them to use the 3 R's – **Receive, Repeat, Respond.**

After the role play, discuss the word choices that worked well and why, and identify any that could have been more helpful or considerate.

ADDITIONAL ACTIVITIES

OPTION 1: SELF-AWARENESS FEELINGS WHEEL

Show students the **Feelings Wheel worksheet**. Ask students to reflect on a recent situation where they felt strong emotions during a conflict. It could be a disagreement with a friend or family member or a frustrating moment at school.

- Ask each student to select an emotion from the wheel that best describes how they felt in that situation.
- In pairs or whole group, ask students to share the emotion they chose and explain why they chose it.
- Discuss how being aware of our emotions can help us communicate more respectfully.

OPTION 2: THOUGHTFUL TEXTING

Using the **Thoughtful Texting worksheet**, have students brainstorm three situations where they might need to communicate a difficult or important message via text (giving feedback, addressing a problem, or questioning a friend). In pairs or small groups, they will choose a situation and create a response, focusing on respectful language.

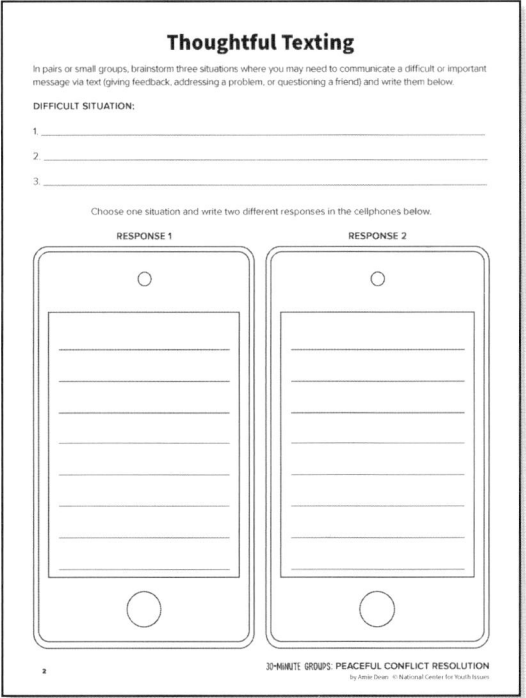

- Encourage students to read and revise their texts and consider whether their word choices could be misunderstood, disrespectful, or sound mean or harsh.
- Students can share their written texts and discuss what helped make the message respectful.

OPTION 3: THINK ACRONYM

Share the **THINK Acronym handout** with students and ask them to discuss which skill/letter they believe they could personally improve during communication. Send it home with students as a resource.

OPTION 4: REFLECTION JOURNAL

Ask students to write, or create a picture, about a recent conversation or situation where they used respectful communication (or where they could have done better). Have them reflect on the following questions:

- How did my words or actions affect the other person?
- Did I listen actively? Was I patient and respectful?
- How could I improve my communication next time?

Afterward, have students pair up and share their reflections. Ask for suggestions for how others could improve communication skills.

CLOSING CONSIDERATIONS

Respectful communication is the first and most important step toward peaceful conflict resolution. The words we choose can make or break our relationships with friends, coworkers, and even family. There is an old saying, "Sticks and stones may break my bones, but words can never hurt me." Many people disagree with this idea and have changed it to say, "Sticks and stones may break my bones, but words can hurt forever." What do you think this means? Being physically hurt may cause a bruise, a broken bone, or even a permanent scar, but we may be able to forget about it once the pain goes away. Words are much harder to forget as the memory of how they made you feel can last a very long time.

If you want to become a better communicator who treats people respectfully, continue to work on your self-awareness so you can make a plan when emotions start to take over. Practice using words that are considerate, honest, and helpful so you can think of them when those emotions show up. Remember that listening without interrupting is an important part of respectful communication. We will focus on active listening in our next session.

Ask students to summarize the content of this session's lesson in one sentence.

Feelings Wheel
(Grades 2-5)

Think about a time recently when you felt big feelings during a problem or disagreement. It could be a disagreement with a friend or family member or a frustrating moment at school. Choose an emotion from the wheel that best describes how you felt.

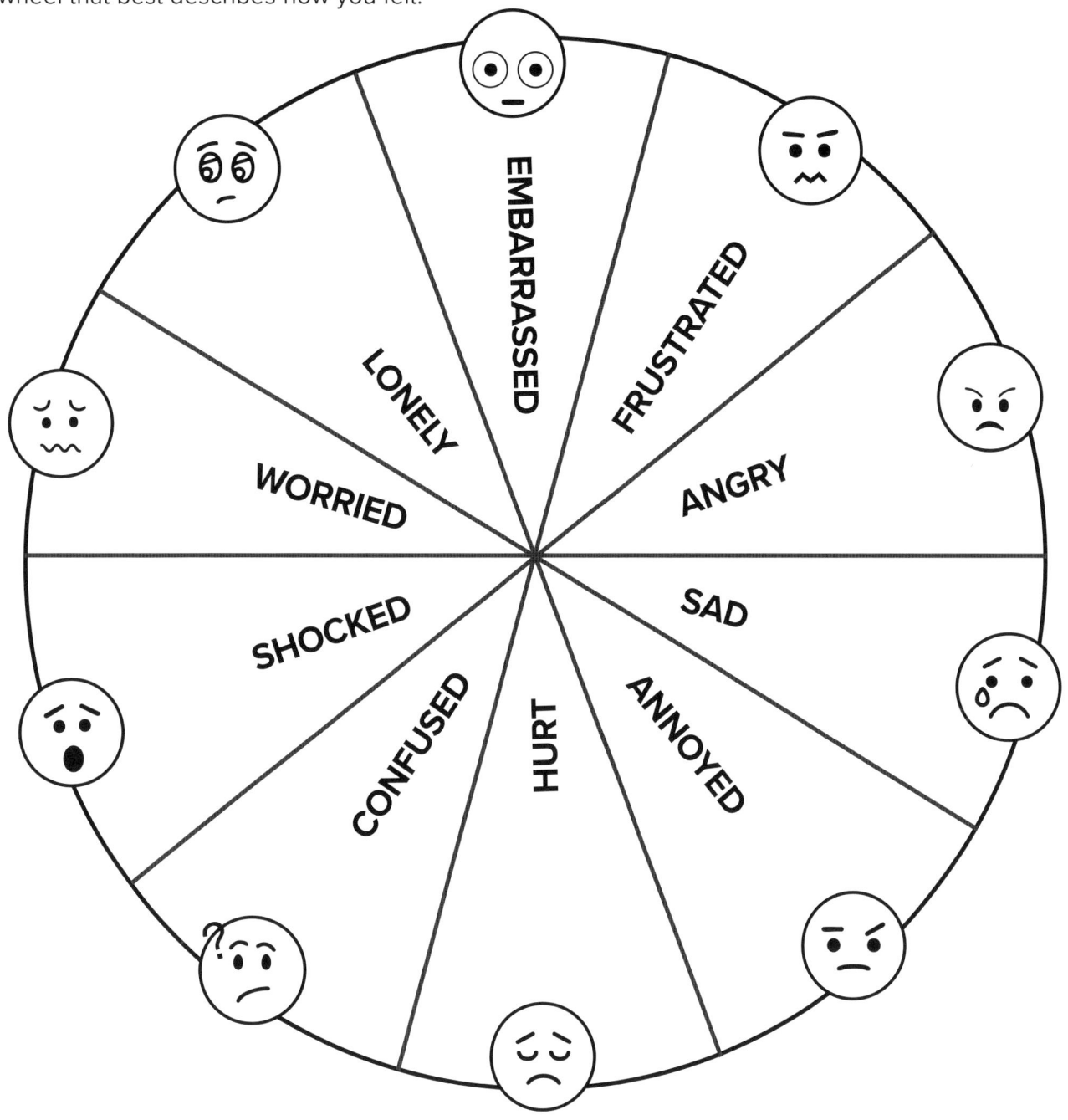

Why did you feel that way? Please explain.

_____

_____

_____

30-MINUTE GROUPS: PEACEFUL CONFLICT RESOLUTION

Feelings Wheel
(Grades 6-8)

Reflect on a recent situation where you felt strong emotions during a conflict. It could be a disagreement with a friend or family member or a frustrating moment at school. Choose an emotion from the wheel that best describes how you felt.

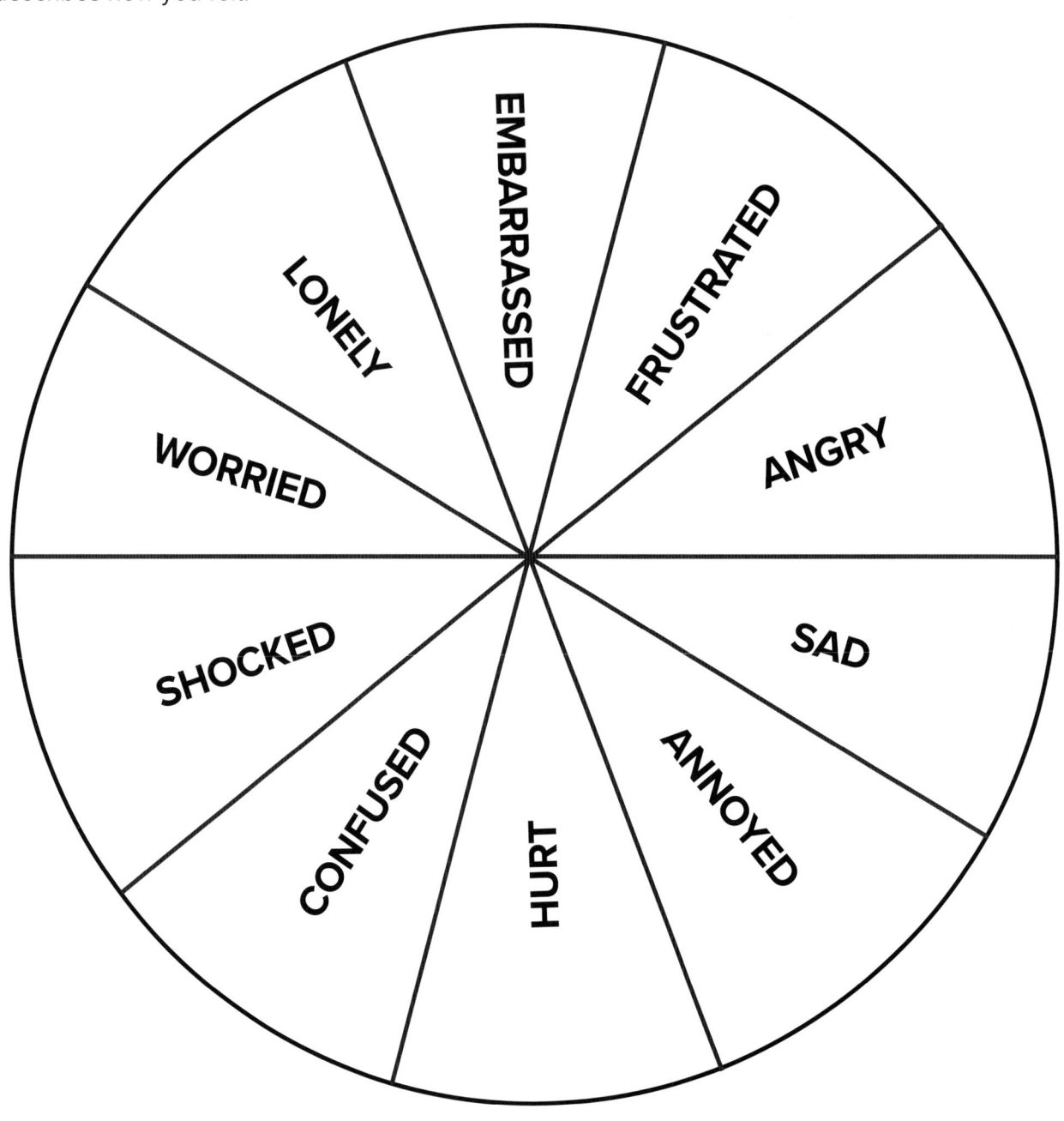

Why did you feel that way? Please explain.

_____
_____
_____

"WHAT WOULD YOU DO - THIS OR THAT?" GAME

Playing the What Would You Do - This or That? Game is a fun and engaging activity for students to develop their critical thinking skills. Students will reflect on their experience, evaluate their options based on their preferences, and reflect on the opinions of others, providing a different perspective and strengthening their sense of connection to one another.

WHAT WOULD YOU DO—THIS OR THAT?

Copy and cut out the questions for small groups to discuss, or have each person stand in the center of the room and move towards one side or the other to show their vote for either option as the facilitator reads the questions aloud.

What would you do if a friend says something hurtful to you in a group chat, but you don't want to make it worse?

- Ignore the message and hope they realize what they did
- Calmly respond, express how you feel and ask for a more respectful tone

What would you do if a classmate disagrees with you in a group project discussion, but starts raising their voice and getting frustrated?

- Start raising your voice back, to make sure your opinion is heard
- Stay calm, listen to their point of view, and ask if you can both talk respectfully so you can figure it out

What would you do if you overheard a friend gossiping about another friend behind their back?

- Join in and add to the gossip because it's easier than speaking up
- Politely tell your friend that gossiping isn't respectful and they should speak directly to your friend

What would you do if someone in your group says something that you disagree with, but you know it could turn into an argument?

- Stay quiet and avoid the conversation to prevent any problems
- Respectfully share your point of view, making sure to listen and speak without getting defensive

What would you do if your best friend cancels plans with you last minute for the third time in a row, and you're feeling frustrated?

- Send a rude text and tell them you're upset
- Send a calm text telling them you feel disappointed and would like to talk about it when they're available

What would you do if a teacher in the hall calls you the wrong name and says you did something you didn't do?

- Raise your voice and tell the teacher they are wrong
- Ask the teacher if you can explain who you are and that you did not do anything wrong.

30-MINUTE GROUPS: PEACEFUL CONFLICT RESOLUTION

Active Listening: The Key to Understanding

MIND MAP

Active Listening – the act of listening to another person, without distractions, to understand what they are trying to say. Active listening includes eye contact, noticing nonverbal cues, and participating without interruption.

On the board, draw a Mind Map, or use the acronym, and ask students to consider the meaning of **Active Listening**.

- Inquire
- Look
- Show
- Active Listening
- Notice
- Empathize
- Think

- **L – Look:** Look at the speaker. Make eye contact and avoid other distractions.
- **I – Inquire:** Ask respectful questions to clarify and help you understand.
- **S – Show:** Show you are listening by nodding or saying "sure" or "I get that."
- **T – Think:** Think before you speak. Consider what they said and choose your words carefully.
- **E – Empathize:** Try to understand their point of view and show that you care about it.
- **N – Notice:** Pay attention to verbal and nonverbal cues such as body language and facial expressions.

ASCA® STANDARDS

- **B-SS 1.** Effective oral and written communication skills and listening skills
- **B-SS 2.** Positive, respectful and supportive relationships with students who are similar to and different from them
- **B-SS 6.** Effective collaboration and cooperation skills

DIRECTIONS

- Review the Group Expectations.
- Conduct a student check-in with the Mood Meter.
- Review and discuss the Mind Map.
- Read the Lesson Introduction and ask the Circle Time Questions.
- Read the Story and follow with Discussion Questions.
- Complete the Skill Practice, What Would You Do – This or That, and Additional Activities as time allows.
- Wrap up with the Closing Considerations for each lesson.

In a small group format, conduct your student check-in using the Mood Meter. Ask students to hold up their number (5, 4, 3, 2, or 1) to show the type of day they are having. Validate each student's number and thank them for sharing. If time, you may ask volunteers to elaborate with one reason they chose their number. Ask the group if they have anything to say to be helpful and encouraging to other group members who shared a 1 or 2 for their check-in. Model kind and uplifting responses for the group each week so they can learn how to respond when a group member is having a tough day.

TEMPERATURE CHECK

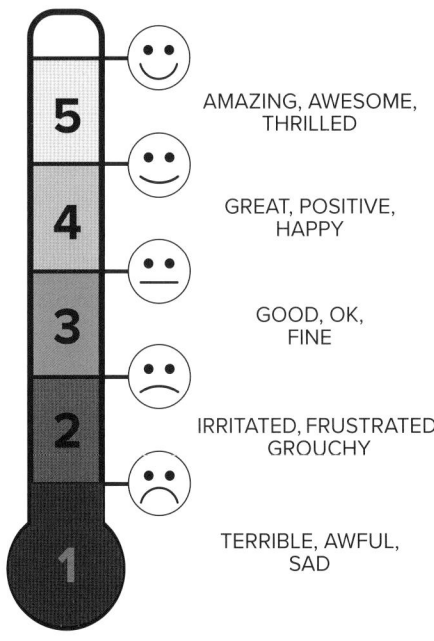

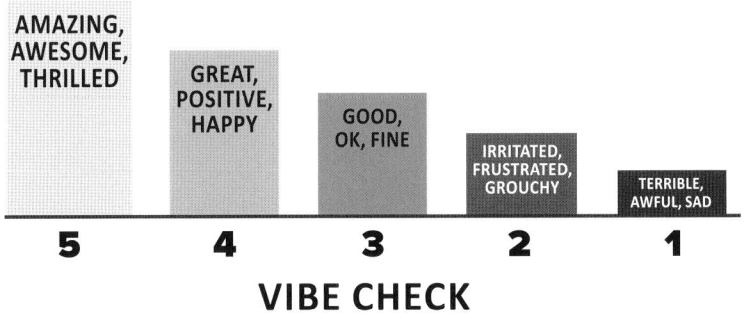

VIBE CHECK

Review the Group Expectations before reviewing the Mind Map. Then, read the Lesson Introduction and ask the Circle Time Questions before reading the Story and the Discussion Questions. Students can work in pairs to craft their responses or share with the whole group. Complete the Skill Practice, What Would You Do - This or That, and Additional Activities as time allows. Be sure to complete the Closing Considerations with each lesson.

LESSON INTRODUCTION

Have you ever felt like someone wasn't listening to you when you were sharing something you were excited about, or something you felt was important? What were they doing that made you feel they weren't listening? We have so many distractions in our lives now with phones, headphones, laptops, hundreds of streaming channels, etc. – it's hard to pay attention!

Many arguments and misunderstandings start because one person didn't really listen to what the other person was saying. Active listening is the practice of making eye contact, ignoring all distractions, and truly listening to another person with the intent of understanding what they are saying – not just hearing the words. What's the difference? We can *hear* the sounds coming from any source without understanding the meaning. Active listening takes effort such as looking, asking questions, participating nonverbally to show interest, and considering the person's point of view. We listen to seek meaning so we can do our part to have respectful communication where people feel heard and valued.

CIRCLE TIME QUESTIONS

Ask students to reflect and share their answers to the following questions with the group. Larger groups may need to be broken into smaller groups to give students ample time to share their answers and deepen the conversation.

- Can you think of a time when you were very excited about something, and you tried to tell a person who wasn't listening? Share what you wanted to say and how that made you feel.
- What do you wish people would do to show you they are listening and interested in what you have to say?
- How can you tell when someone is not listening to you?
- What do you do that you think makes you a good, or not so good, listener?

STORY TIME

Hand out the coloring sheet and crayons or markers while the facilitator reads the story, if desired.

Pizzas and Parts

> It was Thursday afternoon, and the robotics club was getting ready for their big project presentation. The group had been working on their robot for weeks, and today was the last day to put everything together and test it out before they headed downtown on Saturday. If they did well, they might even get a spot in the regional competition.

"Hey, Gavin," Ethan called out, finding his friend at the lockers. "We need to make sure we have all the parts and pieces for the robot at the meeting today. I'm bringing the tools, and we need you to bring sensors, wires, and the power pack, okay?"

Gavin, who was distracted by a text message on his phone, nodded. "Yeah, yeah, got it," he said, barely looking up from his screen. "Sensors, pieces, power pack. Got it."

Ethan raised an eyebrow. "You sure? We can't forget anything. It's super important."

"I'm good, don't worry," Gavin replied, still staring at his phone. "I'll bring them all."

That afternoon, after school, the robotics club met in the science lab for their meeting. Ethan set up his toolbox and started unpacking the tools they would need. A few other members arrived early and started working on the robot. The stress in the room was high; everyone wanted the build to go smoothly.

Gavin walked in a few minutes later holding two large boxes. He walked over to Ethan, who was deep in concentration.

Ethan looked up. "You bring everything?" he asked.

Gavin set the boxes down and smiled. "Yep! Got the goods."

Ethan's eyes widened as he glanced at the boxes. "Wait, what's this?" He opened one box to reveal a large pizza inside.

Gavin laughed. "What? You said to bring pizzas, right?"

Ethan's face went pale. "No, I said *parts and pieces*—sensors, wires, and the power pack! Not *pizzas*!" He grabbed his head in disbelief. "We needed those parts to finish the robot, Gavin! The competition is in less than 48 hours!"

Gavin blinked, looking genuinely confused. "Wait, I thought you said pizzas? That's why I brought two. You know, for everyone to eat while we work on the robot."

Ethan felt the panic start to rise. "I said *pieces*, not pizza! You didn't hear me right because you weren't listening!"

The rest of the group began to notice the situation. There was a mix of confusion and frustration in the room as Ethan paced back and forth. "We need those parts, Gavin! The sensors and wires—those are what power the robot! Without them, we can't even get started!"

Gavin looked down at the pizza boxes and sighed. "Oh man, I thought I heard you say pizza. I guess I wasn't really listening. My bad, Ethan."

Ethan's shoulders slumped. "This is bad, really bad. We're running out of time, and now we're stuck."

At that moment, Briana, another member of the club, spoke up. "Hold on, we still have some spare sensors from the last project. I think we can make it work."

Ethan turned to Briana, trying to hold onto a bit of hope. "Are you sure? We only have an hour before school closes for the night!"

Briana shrugged. "It won't be perfect, but we can get it running. If we can get everything connected, we will have something to show."

The rest of the meeting was intense, but with everyone focused, the group managed to piece together a working version of the robot. It moved, but it didn't have all the sensors they had planned to show off.

When they finally presented the robot at the competition, it wasn't a total disaster, but they knew they could have done better if Gavin had listened and brought what they needed.

Later that day, Ethan pulled Gavin aside. "You know, if you had really been listening to me, we would've been way ahead. We could've done so much more with that time."

Gavin looked down, and his face turned red with embarrassment. "I know, I messed up. I didn't take it seriously enough. Next time, I promise I'll listen carefully. No more phone obsession."

Ethan nodded, "It's alright. Just remember we need you to lock in, especially when everyone's counting on you. It's not just about hearing what people say but making sure you really listen and understand."

Gavin slowly smiled. "Got it, loud and clear. No more pizza mix-ups."

DISCUSSION QUESTIONS

- How did Gavin's distraction impact his robotics team? What could have been different?
- Why is it important to listen to directions when working on something?
- How do you think Ethan felt when he realized that the parts weren't available?
- What would you have done if you were Ethan?
- Have you ever experienced a misunderstanding that had an impact on you?

SKILL PRACTICE

For this Skill Practice, put students in pairs and have them take turns being the speaker and listener. You may want to hand out paper for those who want to take notes.

- **Dream Vacation:** The speaker has 60-90 seconds to describe what their dream vacation would include without giving any locations. Share things such as weather, activities, and what you hope to see at this destination. The listener should actively listen, take notes if preferred, and then suggest a few places where the speaker could go to find their dream vacation.
- **My Favorite Dessert:** The speaker has 60-90 seconds to describe how to make their favorite dessert, what it looks like, where you can get it, and any special toppings or flavors. The listener will actively listen and try to describe the dessert with all the details back to the speaker. NO notes for this one.
- **My Family Tradition:** The speaker will explain a tradition that their family has for a holiday, birthday, or any other event with details. The listener will actively listen with eye contact, nonverbal cues such as nodding or quick comments, and then respond with questions and/or repeating what they heard.

Discuss with the group what they found difficult or easy while actively listening to the speaker.

ADDITIONAL ACTIVITIES

OPTION 1: TELEPHONE GAME

Students sit or stand in a circle. The teacher whispers a short sentence or phrase into the first student's ear (ex. "The dog is wearing a red collar and a blue sweater because it is freezing outside."). That student then whispers the message to the next student, and this continues around the circle. The last student says the message aloud, and everyone compares it to the original. Discuss with the class how misunderstanding someone's words can impact the outcome of a conversation.

OPTION 2: SIMON SAYS

This quick game can be modified to focus on listening carefully to instructions. In this version, the teacher will make the commands more difficult by adding steps (ex. "Simon says touch your nose with your left hand and then clap twice.") The teacher has to say, "Simon Says" before the command for it to be valid. Students must listen actively and follow only the commands that start with "Simon Says." If they perform a command without hearing "Simon Says," they are out. This reinforces the importance of actively listening for specific details and focusing on the speaker.

OPTION 3: SILENT SUMMARY

Pair up students. One student will speak for two minutes about a topic that is important to them. It could be a hobby, a personal experience, or something they're passionate about. The other student must listen without interrupting, judging, or giving advice. The listener should then share a quick summary of what was said. After two minutes, switch roles. After the activity, lead a group discussion about how it felt to be truly listened to without interruption. Ask students to share how it impacted the conversation and their understanding of the other person.

CLOSING CONSIDERATIONS

Active listening is an important skill for peaceful conflict resolution because it leads to respectful communication, promotes understanding, and strengthens relationships. Whether in a classroom, at home, or with your friends, truly listening to others, by making eye contact and focusing on their words, helps prevent misunderstandings and creates an environment where everyone feels valued. The next time you're having a conversation, focus on listening carefully to the other person. Listening is just as important as speaking clearly, and it is the key to understanding. All of us want to feel like what we say is important and that we matter to those who are listening.

Ask students to summarize the content of this session's lesson in one sentence.

"WHAT WOULD YOU DO - THIS OR THAT?" GAME

Playing the What Would You Do - This or That? Game is a fun and engaging activity for students to develop their critical thinking skills. Students will reflect on their experience, evaluate their options based on their preferences, and reflect on the opinions of others, providing a different perspective and strengthening their sense of connection to one another.

What Would You Do–This or That?

Copy and cut out the questions for small groups to discuss, or have each person stand in the center of the room and move towards one side or the other to show their vote for either option as the facilitator reads the questions aloud.

What would you do when the art teacher explains how to do an activity?
- You put down the supplies and listen before touching anything
- You pick up a pencil and paint brushes and start planning your piece of art

What would you do if your parents told you the plan for after-school activities this week?
- You keep playing your video game and trying to listen
- You pause and give them eye contact and add details for the week to your phone

What would you do when your teacher goes over the details of a group project?
- You and your group members start discussing who will do what job
- You listen quietly and wait until the teacher is finished and then start assigning jobs

What would you do when a friend tells you about a problem that made her very upset?
- You listen while watching a video on YouTube, looking at her occasionally
- You stop watching, put your tablet away, and look at her while you listen

What would you do when a new student is telling the class about themselves?
- You look at the new student and wait to raise your hand to ask a question
- You wave your hand in the air while whispering your question to your friend next to you

What would you do while the teacher is explaining the steps to solve a problem after you've asked for help?
- You put your pencil down and look and listen while he explains
- You draw on your paper and repeat, "I just don't get it," over and over

> "One of the most sincere forms of respect is actually listening to what another has to say."
> BRYANT H. MCGILL

NONVERBAL COMMUNICATION: WHAT ARE YOU REALLY SAYING?

MIND MAP

Nonverbal Communication – the process of conveying messages without using words; using visual cues, vocal cues, and other physical behaviors

On the board, draw a Mind Map and ask students to consider the meaning of **Nonverbal Communication.**

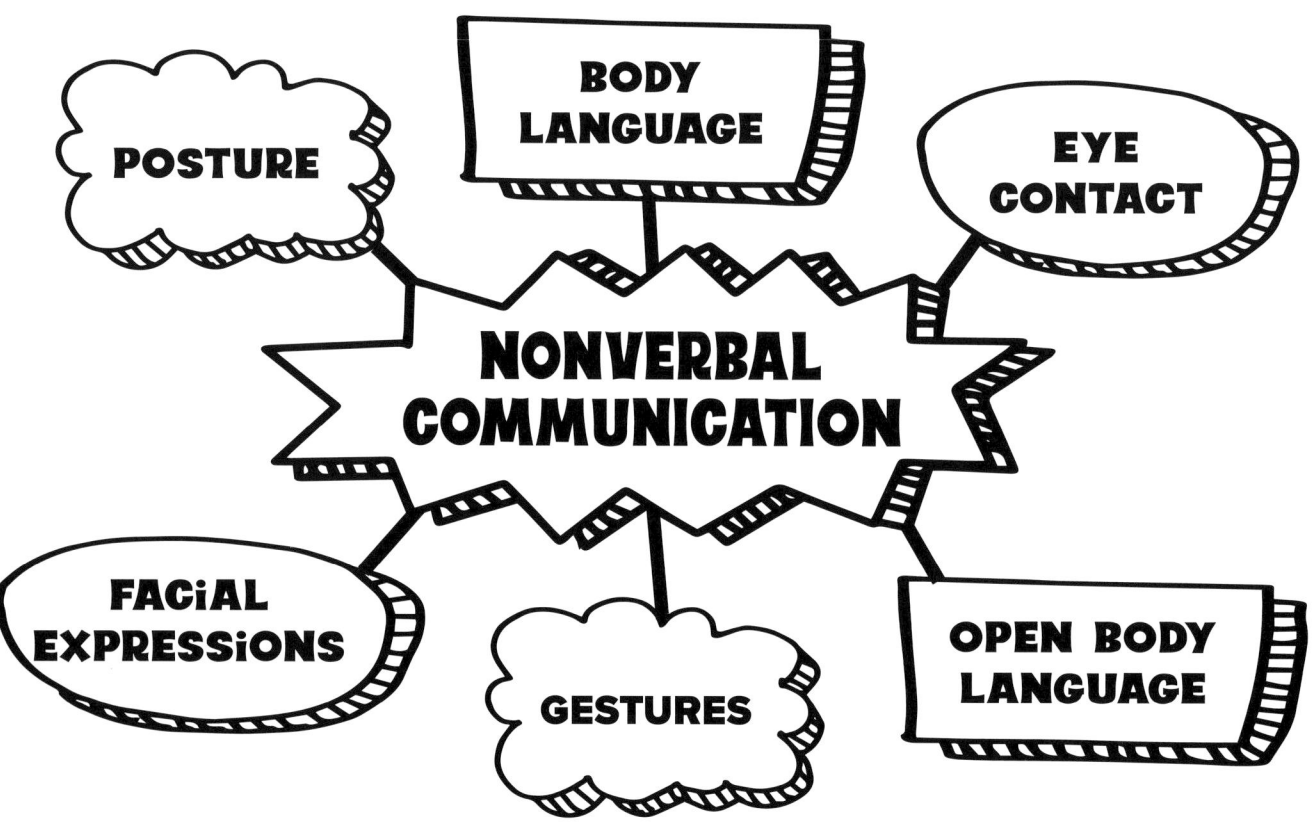

- **Body Language** – how we move our body to show how we feel, like crossed arms, covering your mouth, or turning your head away from the person speaking
- **Open Body Language** – shows signs of being calm and ready to engage such as relaxed face, smiling, eye contact, arms hanging down, hands open
- **Eye Contact** – looking at someone's eyes which can show attentiveness, interest, confidence, or respect
- **Facial Expressions** – the way our face looks to show feelings; smiling, frowning, or eye rolling
- **Gestures** – Hand or arm movements such as waving, pointing, or balling a fist
- **Posture** – The way we sit or stand like sitting up straight to show listening or bending over to show pain

ASCA® STANDARDS

- **B-SS 1.** Effective oral and written communication skills and listening skills
- **B-SS 6.** Effective collaboration and cooperation skills
- **B-SS 9.** Social maturity and behaviors appropriate to the situation and environment

DIRECTIONS

- Review the Group Expectations.
- Conduct a student check-in with the Mood Meter.
- Review and discuss the Mind Map.
- Read the Lesson Introduction and ask the Circle Time Questions.
- Read the Story and follow with Discussion Questions.
- Complete the Skill Practice, What Would You Do – This or That, and Additional Activities as time allows.
- Wrap up with the Closing Considerations for each lesson.

In a small group format, conduct your student check-in using the Mood Meter. Ask students to hold up their number (5, 4, 3, 2, or 1) to show the type of day they are having. Validate each student's number and thank them for sharing. If time, you may ask volunteers to elaborate with one reason they chose their number. Ask the group if they have anything to say to be helpful and encouraging to other group members who shared a 1 or 2 for their check-in. Model kind and uplifting responses for the group each week so they can learn how to respond when a group member is having a tough day.

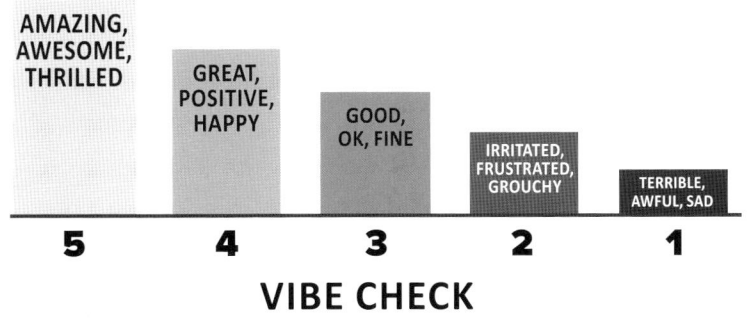

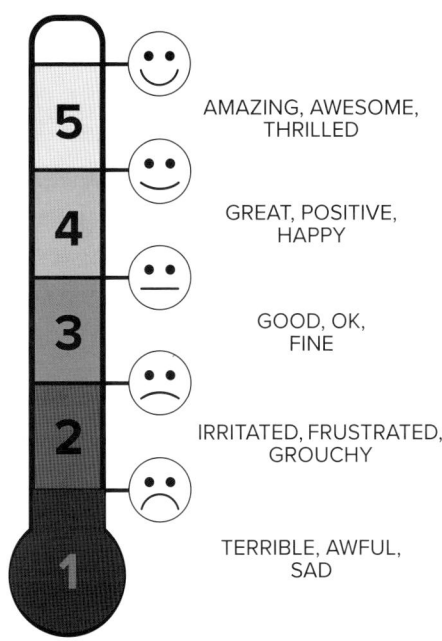

Review the Group Expectations before reviewing the Mind Map. Then, read the Lesson Introduction and ask the Circle Time Questions before reading the Story and the Discussion Questions. Students can work in pairs to craft their responses or share with the whole group. Complete the Skill Practice, What Would You Do - This or That, and Additional Activities as time allows. Be sure to complete the Closing Considerations with each lesson.

LESSON INTRODUCTION

Communication is more than just the words we speak; it's also about how we say them and what we do without speaking. Have you ever tried to hide how you really feel by saying "I'm fine" when you weren't? Or maybe you've seen someone say one thing, but their body language said something completely different? It's often said that "the body never lies," meaning our movements, facial expressions, gestures, and posture can reveal our true emotions, even when we try to hide them. Sometimes a small disagreement can quickly turn into a bigger conflict because of how someone's nonverbal cues are misunderstood – or purposely intended.

In this session, we'll talk about the importance of self-awareness and how the messages we send through body language and facial expressions can influence how others see us. Understanding your nonverbal communication will help you manage your emotions and reactions, making it easier to avoid conflict and communicate peacefully.

CIRCLE TIME QUESTIONS

Ask students to reflect and share their answers to the following questions with the group. Larger groups may need to be broken into smaller groups to give students ample time to share their answers and deepen the conversation.

- Share two or three ways that people can show emotion using their face or body.
- How can misunderstanding someone's nonverbal cues lead to a conflict or disagreement?
- Why is it important to pay attention to other people's nonverbal cues when communicating?
- When someone is told they have a "bad attitude," what kind of body language could they be showing?
- Can you think of a time you were able to tell a friend or family member was upset with you without them saying anything? How did you know?

STORY TIME

Hand out the Coloring Sheets and crayons or markers to younger students while the facilitator reads the story, if desired.

Silent Signals

Farrah and Kylie were sitting together in the courtyard after lunch, talking about their weekend plans. Farrah was excited to tell Kylie about her hiking trip, but she noticed Kylie wasn't really paying attention. Kylie was looking at her tablet and not making eye contact.

"Hey, Kylie, did you hear me?" Farrah asked, tapping her friend's shoulder.

"Yeah, I heard," Kylie said, but she didn't look up from her tablet.

Farrah felt annoyed. Kylie wasn't acting like herself. "Are you mad at me?" Farrah asked, trying to understand.

Kylie looked surprised. "No, I'm not mad. Why would I be?"

Farrah frowned. "You just seem … upset."

Kylie crossed her arms and looked away. "I'm just tired, okay? Can you stop bothering me?"

Farrah didn't understand. She thought Kylie was mad—especially when she crossed her arms and was not looking at her. Farrah's feelings were hurt, and she snapped, "Why are you being like this? I'm just trying to talk to you!"

Kylie stood up, frustrated. "You're the one being rude! I'm just having a bad day!"

As Kylie walked off, Farrah shouted after her, "Fine, I'll leave you alone!"

The argument caused a few other students to stop and watch. Farrah stood there, upset, while Kylie sat alone on a swing.

Stella and Cooper, two other students who had seen the argument, noticed what had happened. Stella walked over to Farrah and said, "Hey, Farrah, Kylie's not mad at you. She's just really worried about her mom and didn't want to talk about it."

Farrah's eyes widened. "Oh, I didn't know that. I thought she was angry at me."

Stella nodded. "I'm sure Kylie didn't mean to make you feel bad. She was just dealing with her stress in her own way."

Farrah felt guilty. "I should go talk to her."

Farrah walked over to Kylie, who was still sitting on the swing. "Kylie, can we talk?"

Kylie nodded and wiped her eyes. "Sure."

"I'm sorry I misunderstood. I thought you were mad at me, but now I know you were just having a tough day," Farrah said.

Kylie smiled a little. "It's okay. I didn't know how to explain it. My mom is really sick, and I don't know what to do."

"I understand. I'm here for you," Farrah said, giving her friend a hug.

DISCUSSION QUESTIONS

- Why do you think Farrah misunderstood Kylie's body language? What could she have done differently to better understand how Kylie was feeling?
- How did Stella help Farrah understand what was really going on with Kylie? What can we learn from Stella's approach to conflict?
- Farrah and Kylie had a misunderstanding because of body language. Can you think of a time when you misjudged someone's body language? What happened, and how did you resolve it?
- Why is it important to pay attention to both what someone says and how they say it (through body language?) How can misreading body language lead to bigger conflicts?
- How can we make sure we don't misjudge someone's body language? What are some good questions to ask to understand how someone is really feeling?

SKILL PRACTICE

Using the round-robin method, go around the table and ask students how they would practice each skill, giving everyone a chance to answer one question. You can adapt this Skill Practice to allow students to respond in pairs or write their answers on paper.

Read each list of gestures, facial expressions, or body language and ask students to share what they or others might interpret with these specific actions:

BODY LANGUAGE	POSSIBLE INTERPRETATIONS
avoiding eye contact, crossing arms, and looking down	Shy, Nervous
jumping, smiling, and spreading arms wide toward someone	Excited, Welcoming
clenching fists, crossing arms, frowning, and breathing fast	Angry
biting nails, fidgeting with clothes, and pacing back and forth	Nervous, Anxious
yawning, slouching, and rubbing eyes	Tired

ADDITIONAL ACTIVITIES

OPTION 1: BODY LANGUAGE CHARADES

Cut out the Body Language Charades Cards. Students take turns drawing a slip and acting out the emotion without using words, only through body language and facial expressions. The other students must guess the emotion or situation being acted out. After each round, discuss how body language was used and if it was effective in communicating the message.

OPTION 2: BODY LANGUAGE ROLE PLAY

This will allow students to practice resolving conflicts in a positive way while paying attention to both verbal and non-verbal cues.

Cut out the **Body Language Role Play Cards**. Split the students into pairs or small groups. Each pair or group will draw a conflict scenario from the stack of cards. The students will act out the conflict twice for each round:

- First, using poor communication (raised voices, angry gestures, crossed arms)
- Next, they will act out the same scenario, but this time using positive conflict resolution strategies (active listening, calm voice, open body language)

Students who are observing can use the **Role Play Feedback Form**.

CLOSING CONSIDERATIONS

Our body language plays an important role in communication and peaceful conflict resolution. The way we stand, sit, or use our hands can send powerful messages, sometimes even more than our words. Understanding body language helps us interpret how others are feeling, but it also reminds us to be mindful of how we express ourselves through non-verbal cues.

Misunderstandings or conflicts often happen when we misread body language. By paying closer attention to both what people say and how they say it, we can keep conflicts from escalating and resolve disagreements peacefully. Practicing positive body language, like open posture, eye contact, and calm gestures, can help us show that we are approachable, respectful, and ready to listen.

Remember, good communication isn't just about what we say—it's also about listening, focusing with our eyes, recognizing emotions, and using our own body language to show empathy and understanding. By applying these skills, we can create stronger, more positive relationships with those around us.

Ask students to summarize the content of this session's lesson in one sentence.

Body Language Charades Cards

HAPPY 	**SAD** 
ANGRY 	**CONFUSED** 
EXCITED 	**ANNOYED** 
FRUSTRATED 	**SURPRISED** 

Body Language Role Play Cards

Someone took your headphones and used them without asking.	You heard another "friend" was talking about the clothes you are wearing.
A group of classmates told you there isn't enough room for you to sit with them at the assembly.	Two friends argue over who gets the last piece of pizza.
A student interrupts another student multiple times while speaking.	A friend tells the teacher you didn't finish your homework for no reason.

Role Play Feedback Form

1. Write a brief description of the situation in each "scenario" box.
2. Describe the nonverbal messages that each actor sent during their role play.
3. Identify the pros and cons for each type of communication for each scenario.

	Negative Body Language – Pros/Cons	**Positive Body Language – Pros/Cons**
Scenario 1:		
Scenario 2:		
Scenario 3:		
Scenario 4:		

30-MINUTE GROUPS: **PEACEFUL CONFLICT RESOLUTION**

"WHAT WOULD YOU DO - THIS OR THAT?" GAME

Playing the What Would You Do - This or That? Game is a fun and engaging activity for students to develop their critical thinking skills. Students will reflect on their experience, evaluate their options based on their preferences, and reflect on the opinions of others, providing a different perspective and strengthening their sense of connection to one another.

WHAT WOULD YOU DO—THIS OR THAT?

Copy and cut out the questions for small groups to discuss, or have each person stand in the center of the room and move towards one side or the other to show their vote for either option as the facilitator reads the questions aloud.

What would you do if your friend has been getting on your nerves?
- Throw your hands up in the air and yell, "get away from me!"
- Make eye contact and let them know in a calm voice that their yelling is making you feel stressed

What would you do if your guardian told you that you cannot go outside because it is after dark?
- Sit down and ask them if you can share your plan for them to walk you halfway and your friend's parents meet you and walk the rest of the way
- Scream, "that's not fair!" and stomp to your room

What would you do if a teacher asked you to stop running as you passed him in the hallway?
- Keep running and yell, "you aren't my teacher!"
- Stop, walk, and say, "I'm sorry" to the teacher

What would you do if a teacher asked if you understand the directions for an activity?
- Turn your head and shrug your shoulders
- Sit up, raise your hand, and ask the teacher to review one more time

What would you do if a student you don't normally sit with asks you to sit with her?
- Smile, nod, and say sure thanks for asking
- Roll your eyes and say, I guess so

What would you do if your basketball coach was giving you feedback at the end of practice?
- Stand still, make eye contact, and nod your head while he talks
- Look down, kick the floor, and stay silent

30-MINUTE GROUPS: PEACEFUL CONFLICT RESOLUTION

FINDING CALM: STRATEGIES FOR MANAGING STRONG EMOTIONS

MIND MAP

Managing Emotions – the ability to identify, understand, and regulate your emotional experiences in a healthy and respectful way

On the board, draw a Mind Map and ask students to consider the meaning of **Managing Emotions.**

- STRESS MANAGEMENT
- SELF-CONTROL
- MINDFULNESS
- MANAGING EMOTIONS
- REFRAMING
- POSITIVE AFFIRMATIONS
- SELF-AWARENESS

30-MINUTE GROUPS: **PEACEFUL CONFLICT RESOLUTION**

- **Mindfulness** – Paying attention to how you feel, your thoughts, and what is going on around you in the present moment
- **Stress Management** – Strategies to handle stress in a healthy way, like deep breathing, physical activity, or talking with someone
- **Self-Awareness** – Knowing what you're feeling and why; understanding your own emotions
- **Self-Control** – The ability to manage your actions, emotions, and words — even when it's hard
- **Reframing** – Looking at a situation in a more positive or helpful way
- **Positive Affirmations** – Kind, encouraging things you say to yourself to help stay confident and calm

ASCA® STANDARDS

- **B-LS 4.** Self-motivation and self-direction for learning
- **B-SMS 2.** Self-discipline and self-control
- **B-SMS 7.** Effective coping skills
- **B-SMS 10.** Ability to manage transitions and adapt to change
- **B-SS 2.** Positive, respectful, and supportive relationships with students

DIRECTIONS

- Review the Group Expectations.
- Conduct a student check-in with the Mood Meter.
- Review and discuss the Mind Map.
- Read the Lesson Introduction and ask the Circle Time Questions.
- Read the Story and follow with Discussion Questions.
- Complete the Skill Practice, What Would You Do – This or That, and Additional Activities as time allows.
- Wrap up with the Closing Considerations for each lesson.

In a small group format, conduct your student check-in using the Mood Meter. Ask students to hold up their number (5, 4, 3, 2, or 1) to show the type of day they are having. Validate each student's number and thank them for sharing. If time, you may ask volunteers to elaborate with one reason they chose their number. Ask the group if they have anything to say to be helpful and encouraging to other group members who shared a 1 or 2 for their check-in. Model kind and uplifting responses for the group each week so they can learn how to respond when a group member is having a tough day.

TEMPERATURE CHECK

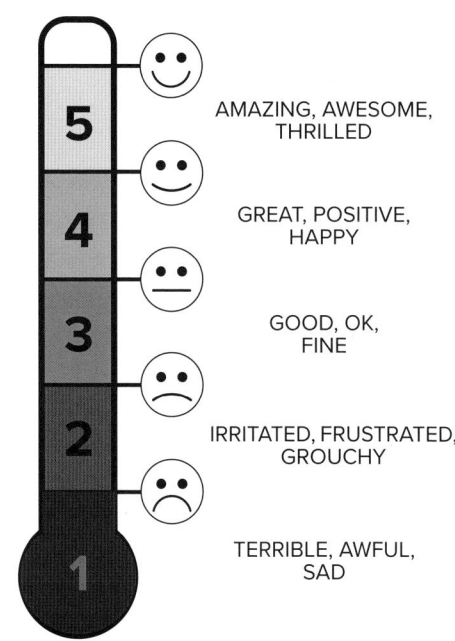

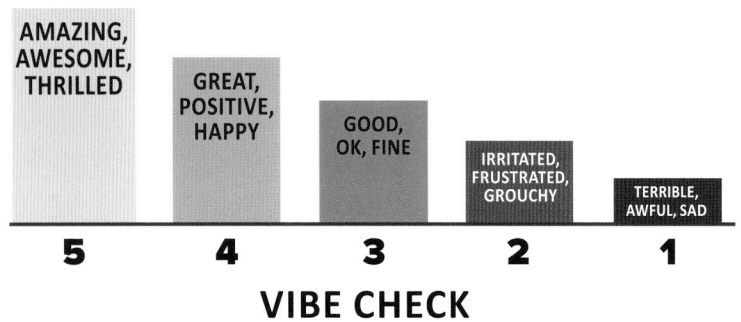

VIBE CHECK

Review the Group Expectations before reviewing the Mind Map. Then, read the Lesson Introduction and ask the Circle Time Questions before reading the Story and the Discussion Questions. Students can work in pairs to craft their responses or share with the whole group. Complete the Skill Practice, What Would You Do - This or That, and Additional Activities as time allows. Be sure to complete the Closing Considerations with each lesson.

LESSON INTRODUCTION

Have you ever felt like your emotions were taking over — maybe feeling so angry you wanted to scream, or so nervous you couldn't think straight? Having big feelings is something we all experience! Emotions are a normal part of life, and everyone feels things like happiness, sadness, stress, and frustration. The most important part of managing our emotions is learning how to understand our feelings and deal with them in healthy ways - even when it is hard to do.

Today, we're going to discuss emotions we all feel sometimes, why they happen, and how we can manage them — especially when things get tough. You'll learn ideas for staying calm during conflict, turning negative thoughts into positive ones, and using strategies to stay in control when your feelings are overwhelming. By understanding and managing our emotions, we can make better choices, feel more confident, and have positive and peaceful relationships in our lives.

(Using the Mood Meter at the beginning of each session is a great example of self-awareness!)

CIRCLE TIME QUESTIONS

Ask students to reflect and share their answers to the following questions with the group. Larger groups may need to be broken into smaller groups to give students ample time to share their answers and deepen the conversation.

- What emotions might you feel when you are in conflict with a friend or family member?
- Do you have any strategies that you have learned or have used in those challenging situations?
- Describe what happens to your body when you get mad or frustrated.
- What makes managing your emotions relevant to peaceful conflict resolution? How are they related?

STORY TIME

Hand out the Coloring Sheets and crayons or markers to younger students while the facilitator reads the story, if desired.

Field Trip Feelings

It was finally here — the 7th-grade field trip to the aquarium! The students had been talking about it for weeks. Everyone piled onto the bus, excited to see the sea creatures and enjoy a whole day away from school. Jamal, Sofia, and Eli were in a group together, and at first, they were all happy about it. They laughed their way through the saltwater exhibit, saw jellyfish that seemed to glow in the dark, and stood in awe when a giant whale shark swam by the glass. But by lunchtime, everyone was tired, hungry, and a little cranky.

"Let's sit over here," Jamal said, pointing to a table near the windows. "It's got the best view."

"No," Sofia said, already walking toward another table. "We should sit near the gift shop so we can get there first after we eat."

"I don't want to sit over there. It's loud and crowded," Jamal said, raising his voice.

"It's not that big of a deal," Sofia snapped. "You don't always have to be in charge!"

Jamal's eyes narrowed. "I'm not trying to be in charge. I just don't want to sit in the middle of a bunch of little kids!"

"Oh my gosh, Jamal. You're so dramatic. Just sit down."

"Why don't *you* sit down and stop bossing everyone around!"

Students nearby were starting to look over. Eli was uncomfortably silent, his sandwich halfway unwrapped. His stomach was tight, and he could feel the tension building with his group. The fun, easy vibe from earlier was gone — and now it felt like the rest of the day might fall apart.

Eli took a slow breath, remembering something their teacher had talked about in class. Mindfulness. Just breathe and notice what's happening, without letting it take over. He focused on his breath — in through the nose, out through the mouth. He glanced at Jamal, whose fists were clenched, then over at Sofia, who looked like she was about to get up and walk away.

"Okay," Eli said, trying to keep his voice steady. "We're all stressed, and we're probably just hangry. Can we take a second before this gets out of control?"

Jamal looked at him, then at Sofia, and then back at the windows. He let out a breath. "Whatever. I just wanted to sit there because I needed a break from the noise."

Sofia sat down at the nearest table and rolled her eyes, but her voice softened. "I wasn't trying to take over. I just wanted to eat and then go shopping."

Eli took another breath. "What if we eat here, and then go hang by the windows after? Both spots, no big deal."

There was a pause. Jamal nodded and sat down next to them. Sofia offered him a chip without saying a word, and things started to feel a little normal again.

Later, as the teacher gathered everyone for a quick end-of-day reflection, she said, "I hope you all enjoyed the trip and had a great time with your groups. I thought the day was just perfect!"

The three friends didn't say much, but they all gave each other a look. It hadn't been a perfect day — but they had figured out how to get through it. And that mattered more than a perfect day.

DISCUSSION QUESTIONS

- What strategy did Eli use to help with the situation?
- Why do you think Jamal and Sofia got so upset?
- What is one example of self-control in the story?
- How did the students resolve their conflict?

SKILL PRACTICE

Using the round-robin method, go around the table and ask students which skill they could use from the Mind Map in each of the scenarios, and ask them to give an example of the skill. You can adapt this Skill Practice to allow students to respond in pairs or write their answers on paper.

Ask students to read each scenario and decide which skill or skills they could apply to help. Skills to consider: **Mindfulness, Stress Management, Self-Awareness, Self-Control, Reframing,** and **Positive Affirmations**

- You're working on a group project in class and one of your teammates keeps ignoring your ideas and talking over you. You're starting to feel frustrated and like your opinion doesn't matter.
- You forgot to bring your homework to school — again — and your teacher is disappointed. You feel embarrassed and upset with yourself.
- Two of your friends are arguing at lunch and you're stuck in the middle. You don't want to pick sides, but the tension is making you anxious and uncomfortable.
- It's game day, and you're super nervous about making a mistake in front of your team. Your hands are sweaty and your heart is racing.
- A friend thinks you were ignoring them on purpose, but you just didn't hear them. Now they're upset and giving you the silent treatment.

ADDITIONAL ACTIVITIES

OPTION 1: MINDSET MAKEOVER

Use the **Mindset Makeover worksheet** or write examples from the group on the board. If you choose to use the worksheet, pass it out. Encourage students to share options to turn their negative thoughts into positive affirmations to help control the stress and strong emotions that come with anxiety or negative self-talk.

- I'm not smart enough.
- I always get things wrong.
- No one likes me.
- I'll never be good at this.
- I can't do anything right.
- I'm a failure.

- This is too hard.
- I give up.
- I'm not as good as everyone else.
- I mess everything up.

OPTION 2: PAUSE – PROCESS – PROCEED

When something makes you feel angry or upsets you quickly, that is called a ***trigger.*** In this activity, you will read examples of common triggers and decide what you would do in each step of the pause – process – proceed method.

- **Pause** – Stop and breathe, count 1-10, picture a peaceful or calming place.
- **Process** – Think about *why* this upsets you and how you can control your emotions – using your thinking brain.
- **Proceed** – Make a decision that allows you to stay in control, stay out of trouble, and work it out.

*For younger students, try Stop-Breathe-Think or the "Turtle Technique"

Examples:

- Someone cuts in line at recess.
- You get left out of a group by your best friend.
- You get picked last for a game.
- Someone laughs at you in front of the class.
- The teacher calls on you when you're not ready.
- You lose a game you really wanted to win.
- Someone takes your seat or supplies.
- A classmate blames you for something.
- You get told no when you ask for something.
- Someone making a rude comment on social media.

OPTION 3: POSITIVE PLAYLIST

Ask students to share songs that help them feel positive, motivated, calm, or powerful. Play a clip of specific songs shared and ask students to talk about how the song helps them.

CLOSING CONSIDERATIONS

Learning to manage strong emotions isn't always easy — but it's one of the most powerful skills we can develop. We've talked about different emotions and challenges and how we can respond to them in ways that help rather than hurt. Whether it's frustration during a conflict, nervousness before a test, or anger when something feels unfair, our feelings are real — and our feelings matter.

The good news is we don't have to let those emotions control us. With tools like deep breathing, positive self-talk, reframing negative thoughts, and practicing self-awareness (like using the Mood Meter) we can stay calm and make better choices — even when emotions feel big. These strategies help us not only feel more in control, but also build stronger relationships, solve conflicts peacefully, and take care of our mental and emotional well-being.

Managing emotions takes practice, and we will all mess up sometimes. Using what we've learned will help you do better and make you more confident that you can handle your emotions when hard things happen. *Your emotions are messages — not mistakes*. Pause, take a breath, and find your calm.

Ask students to summarize the content of this session's lesson in one sentence.

Mindset Makeover

Turn each Negative Thought below into a Positive Thought.

NEGATIVE THOUGHT	POSITIVE THOUGHT
"I'm not smart enough."	
"I always get things wrong."	
"No one likes me."	
"I'll never be good at this."	
"I can't do anything right."	
"I'm a failure."	
"This is too hard."	
"I give up."	
"I'm not as good as everyone else."	
"I mess everything up."	

"WHAT WOULD YOU DO - THIS OR THAT?" GAME

Playing the What Would You Do - This or That? Game is a fun and engaging activity for students to develop their critical thinking skills. Students will reflect on their experience, evaluate their options based on their preferences, and reflect on the opinions of others, providing a different perspective and strengthening their sense of connection to one another.

WHAT WOULD YOU DO—THIS OR THAT?

Copy and cut out the questions for small groups to discuss, or have each person stand in the center of the room and move towards one side or the other to show their vote for either option as the facilitator reads the questions aloud.

How would you choose to manage stress or challenging emotions?
- Take a 10-minute mindfulness break during a stressful day
- Power through and finish early but feel drained

How would you choose to manage stress or challenging emotions?
- Say a positive affirmation every morning
- Write down three things you're grateful for each night

How would you choose to manage stress or challenging emotions?
- Pause and breathe before reacting in a heated moment
- Speak your mind immediately and risk saying something you regret

How would you choose to manage stress or challenging emotions?
- Reframe a failure as a learning opportunity
- Avoid trying to prevent failure in the first place

How would you choose to manage stress or challenging emotions?
- Journal your emotions daily
- Talk them out with a trusted person once a week

How would you choose to manage stress or challenging emotions?
- Deal with stress by exercising for 30 minutes
- Binge-watch your favorite show for an hour

"WHAT WOULD YOU DO - THIS OR THAT?" GAME

CHAPTER 7

Empathy in Action: Walking in Someone Else's Shoes

MIND MAP

Empathy – the ability to understand and share the feelings of another; being sensitive to how others feel

On the board, draw a Mind Map and ask students to consider the meaning of **Empathy.**

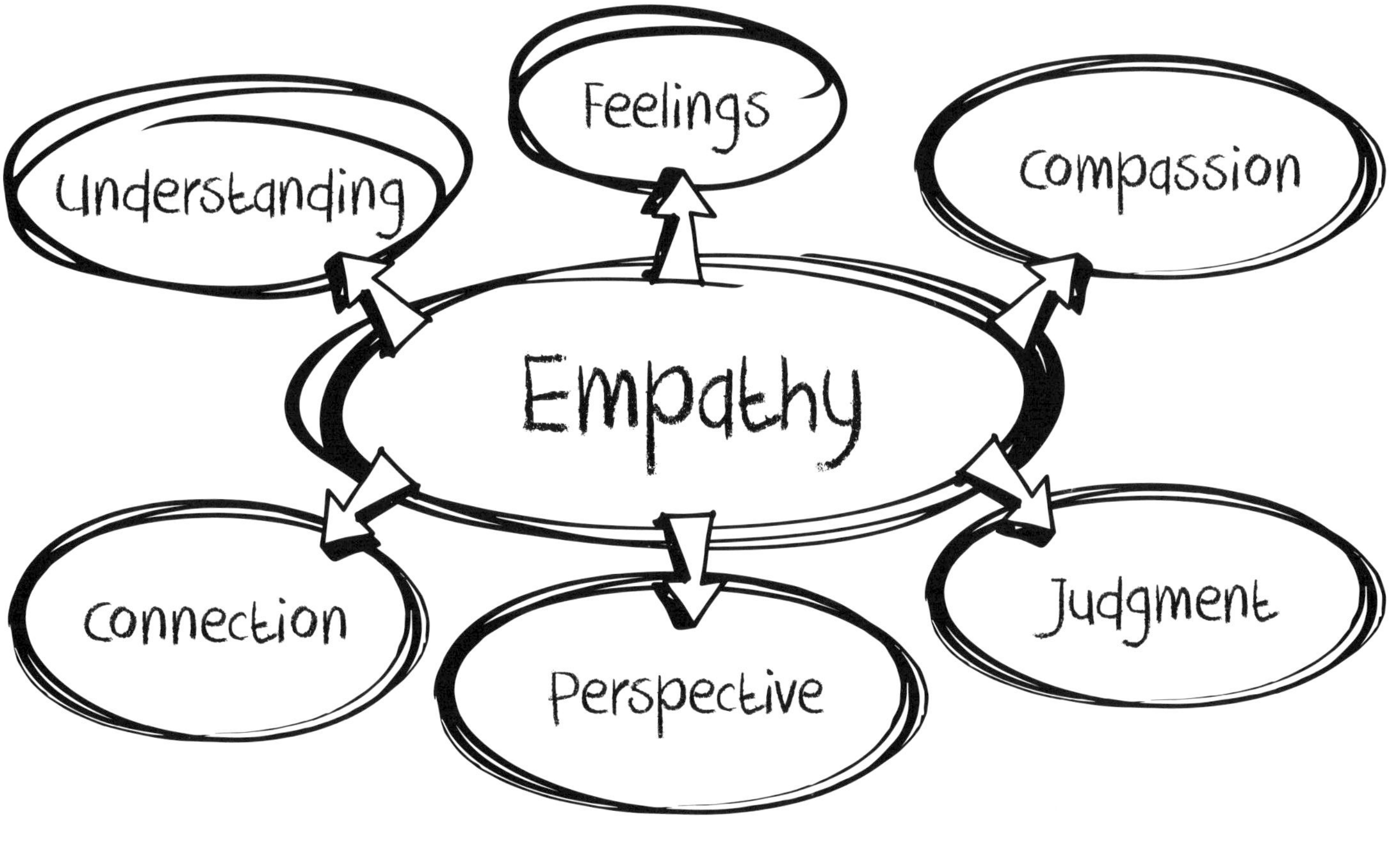

Feelings
Understanding
compassion
Empathy
connection
Judgment
Perspective

- **Feelings** – the emotions that we have like happiness, excitement, anger, fear
- **Compassion** – feeling concern or sorrow for someone's suffering and wanting to help
- **Connection** – the bond we build with others when we understand and care about what they are going through
- **Understanding** – grasping the facts and circumstances of another person's situation, thoughts, or feelings
- **Perspective** – a way of looking at or thinking about something; your point of view
- **Judgment** – criticizing someone instead of trying to understand their experience

ASCA® STANDARDS

- **B-LS 9.** Decision-making informed by gathering evidence, getting others' perspectives and recognizing personal bias
- **B-SS 2.** Positive, respectful, and supportive relationships with other students
- **B-SS 4.** Demonstrates empathy

DIRECTIONS

- Review the Group Expectations.
- Conduct a student check-in with the Mood Meter.
- Review and discuss the Mind Map.
- Read the Lesson Introduction and ask the Circle Time Questions.
- Read the Story and follow with Discussion Questions.
- Complete the Skill Practice, Would You Rather?, and Additional Activities as time allows.
- Wrap up with the Closing Considerations for each lesson.

In a small group format, conduct your student check-in using the Mood Meter. Ask students to hold up their number (5, 4, 3, 2, or 1) to show the type of day they are having. Validate each student's number and thank them for sharing. If time, you may ask volunteers to elaborate with one reason they chose their number. Ask the group if they have anything to say to be helpful and encouraging to other group members who shared a 1 or 2 for their check-in. Model kind and uplifting responses for the group each week so they can learn how to respond when a group member is having a tough day.

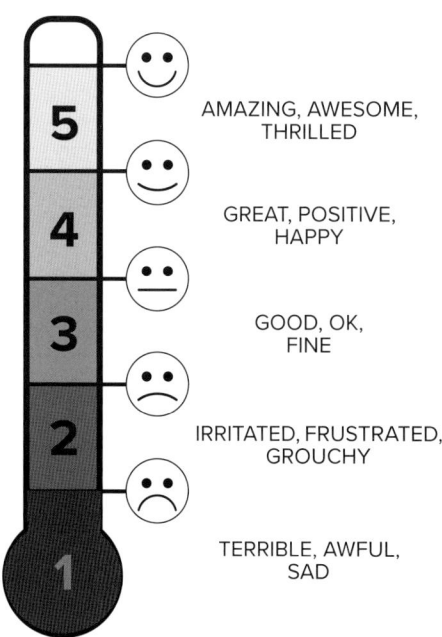

TEMPERATURE CHECK

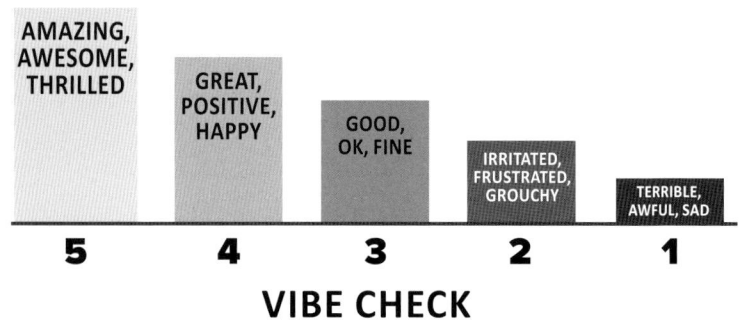

VIBE CHECK

30-MINUTE GROUPS: PEACEFUL CONFLICT RESOLUTION

Review the Group Expectations before reviewing the Mind Map. Then, read the Lesson Introduction and ask the Circle Time Questions before reading the Story and the Discussion Questions. Students can work in pairs to craft their responses or share with the whole group. Complete the Skill Practice, Would You Rather?, and Additional Activities as time allows. Be sure to complete the Closing Considerations with each lesson.

LESSON INTRODUCTION

Can you think of a time when you felt left out and nobody noticed? Maybe you were sad, frustrated, or just needed a friend. Now try to imagine someone else feeling the same way you did, and you are the one who could be a friend. That is what empathy, or being empathetic, looks like.

Empathy means trying to understand what someone else is going through by imagining what it's like to be them. You put aside your own feelings and thoughts for a moment and try to understand theirs. You might have heard the saying, "Take a walk in someone else's shoes," but that doesn't mean you will really trade shoes! It's trying to see things from their perspective which means seeing through their eyes and not just your own.

When we show empathy, we become better friends, better classmates, and better people. It helps us listen more, judge less, and treat others the way *we* would want to be treated. When we feel that others care about us, we can move forward through conflict or disagreements more peacefully. Whether someone is happy, worried, excited, or upset, empathy helps us connect and show kindness, no matter the situation.

CIRCLE TIME QUESTIONS

Ask students to reflect and share their answers to the following questions with the group. Larger groups may need to be broken into smaller groups to give students ample time to share their answers and deepen the conversation.

- What does "walking in someone else's shoes" mean to you?
- How does it feel when someone shows kindness or listens to you when you're having a hard day?
- Have you ever said or done something and then realized later it hurt someone's feelings? What could you have done differently to show more empathy?
- What does it mean to be judgmental? Have you ever felt like you were being judged for something?
- How does showing empathy help us avoid conflict or arguments?

STORY TIME

Hand out the Coloring Sheets and crayons or markers to younger students while the facilitator reads the story, if desired.

The New Kid

The students were sitting in math class waiting for Ms. Johnson to come in and get started. It seemed like it was just another Monday—until Ms. Johnson walked in with a new student.

"This is Leo," she said, smiling. "He just moved here and will be in our class."

Leo barely smiled and then stared at the floor. Noah noticed his clothes looked a little different, and he spoke with an accent when he answered Ms. Johnson.

At lunch, Leo sat by himself. Some kids whispered and giggled. Noah wasn't sure what to do. He felt bad, but he didn't want to leave his group. Then he remembered what it felt like when he was the new kid two years ago —how nervous he was, and how much he wished someone had talked to him.

So, Noah stood up, walked over to Leo's table, and asked, "Wanna come sit with us?" Leo's eyes lit up, and he smiled for the first time that day.

"I remember what it was like when I first moved here," Noah said. "Everything felt different, and I didn't really know anyone. It finally got better when I met some people. That made it easier to come to school."

Leo looked up, "Yeah, I don't know anyone yet. I've been dreading coming to a new school."

"I get that," Noah said. "But I'm sure you'll make friends."

The next day, Noah saw Leo sitting alone again. This time, Noah didn't wait. He got up from his seat and walked right over to Leo's table again.

"Hey, Leo! You want to join us?" Noah asked, smiling.

Leo hesitated, then shook his head. "Sure. Thanks."

As they walked to Noah's table, Leo opened up a little more. "I moved here from a different city, and it's hard to make new friends. My old school was really different, and I miss my friends there."

Noah nodded, understanding. "I know exactly what you mean. But the more you hang out with us, the more you'll get to know everyone. It just takes time."

By the end of the week, Leo was starting to smile more and even laugh at some of the jokes his new classmates made. Noah introduced him to other kids and invited him to play soccer during break. Slowly, Leo was starting to feel like part of the group, and Noah felt good, knowing that he had helped make Leo feel welcome.

One afternoon, after school, Leo caught up with Noah as he was headed to the bus. "Hey, Noah," Leo said quietly, "I just wanted to say thank you for sitting with me that first day. It really helped me."

Noah smiled and said, "I remember how it felt to be the new kid, so I'm glad I could help."

Leo laughed. "Yeah, I still miss my old school, but I think I'm going to like it here."

DISCUSSION QUESTIONS

- How do you think Leo felt on his first day at the new school? Why?
- Why do you think Noah decided to leave his table and ask Leo to sit with him?
- Can you think of a time when someone showed you kindness, just like Noah did for Leo? How did it make you feel?
- What are some ways you can show empathy to someone who might be feeling left out or nervous?

SKILL PRACTICE

Using the round-robin method, go around the table and ask students how they would practice each skill, giving everyone a chance to answer one question. You can adapt this Skill Practice to allow students to respond in pairs or write their answers on paper.

- During PE, teams are being picked for a basketball game, and one student is the last to be picked. They look disappointed and left out.
  How can you show empathy in this situation, even if you're already on a team?
- You're in a group chat with friends when one of them starts making fun of someone who isn't in the chat. A few people laugh and add more comments.
  How can you respond with empathy—even if it's awkward or uncomfortable?
- A student you don't really know is trying to join your group project, but the rest of your group already knows each other and are ignoring the new kid.
  What could you say or do to show empathy to the newer student?
- Your sibling broke their foot and cannot swim on the family vacation.
  What can you do to show compassion or caring to your sibling?

ADDITIONAL ACTIVITIES

OPTION 1: SHOW YOU C.A.R.E.

Using the **C.A.R.E. handout,** show the students the C.A.R.E acronym and discuss the four steps to showing empathy using C.A.R.E. Put students in groups and give each group a scenario. First, they will use the **Show You C.A.R.E. worksheet** to plan each step. Then, they will act out the scenario with all four of the steps shown in their skit.

- **C** – **Connect** with the person (listen and give them your attention)
- **A** – **Acknowledge** their feelings (show you know what they're feeling)
- **R** – **Respond** with kindness (use kind words, a calm tone, positive body language)
- **E** – **Encourage** (offer support or help them feel stronger)

Scenarios:

- A student forgot their lunch and is upset and hungry.
- A student fell in the hallway in front of everyone and is embarrassed.
- A friend's pet died, and they are very sad.
- A student is sitting alone at recess.

OPTION 2: EMPATHY JOURNAL: WALK IN THEIR SHOES

Students choose a person (real or imaginary) and write a short journal entry from that person's point of view. Topics to choose from:

- What would your day be like if you were a new student?
- What could a student with a broken arm be thinking and feeling today?
- A student with special needs is being teased every day. What would it feel like to be them?
- Your teacher called on your friend to read out loud, and he struggled. How does he feel?

CLOSING CONSIDERATIONS

Empathy is about more than just noticing when someone is sad or upset—it's about trying to feel what they're feeling, even if we haven't been through the same thing. When we use empathy, we're seeing the world from another person's perspective, and that helps us connect with others in a kind and respectful way.

Showing empathy can also help us solve problems peacefully. When we take the time to understand how someone else feels, we're more likely to talk things out instead of arguing. By listening and thinking about others' feelings, we can turn conflict into conversation. That's how empathy leads to compassion and better choices. It helps us treat others with care and find solutions that make everyone feel heard and respected.

Ask students to summarize the content of this session's lesson in one sentence.

Show Someone You C.A.R.E.

CONNECT with the person (listen and give them your attention)

ACKNOWLEDGE their feelings (show you know what they're feeling)

RESPOND with kindness (use kind words, a calm tone, positive body language)

ENCOURAGE (offer support or help them feel stronger)

Show You C.A.R.E.

Divide into groups and use this worksheet to plan each CARE step for the scenarios below. When finished, plan a skit acting act out one scenario with all four of the CARE steps.

> **C – Connect** with the person (listen and give them your attention)
> **A – Acknowledge** their feelings (show you know what they're feeling)
> **R – Respond** with kindness (use kind words, a calm tone, positive body language)
> **E – Encourage** (offer support or help them feel stronger)

A student forgot their lunch and is upset and hungry.

Connect _____

Acknowledge _____

Respond _____

Encourage _____

A student fell in the hallway in front of everyone and is embarrassed.

Connect _____

Acknowledge _____

Respond _____

Encourage _____

A friend's pet died and they are very sad.

Connect _____

Acknowledge _____

Respond _____

Encourage _____

A student is sitting alone at recess.

Connect _____

Acknowledge _____

Respond _____

Encourage _____

"WOULD YOU RATHER?" GAME

Playing the Would You Rather? Game is a fun and engaging activity for students to develop their critical thinking skills. Students will reflect on their experience, evaluate their options based on their preferences, and reflect on the opinions of others, providing a different perspective and strengthening their sense of connection to one another.

Would You Rather?

Copy and cut out the questions for small groups to discuss, or have each person stand in the center of the room and move towards one side or the other to show their vote for either option as the facilitator reads the questions aloud.

Would you rather:
- Have a friend who always listens to you
- Be the friend who always helps others feel better

Would you rather:
- Feel someone else's emotions for a day
- Have someone feel your emotions for a day

Would you rather:
- Have one best friend who understands you completely
- Have lots of friends who are kind but don't fully get you

Would you rather:
- Be able to see things from anyone's perspective anytime
- Be able to help someone feel better just by talking to them

Would you rather:
- Have a superpower that lets you fix problems between friends
- Have a superpower that helps people understand each other better

Would you rather:
- Know how to listen well to someone who is upset
- Know what to say to someone who is upset

30-MINUTE GROUPS: PEACEFUL CONFLICT RESOLUTION

> *"Learning to stand in somebody else's shoes, to see through their eyes, that's how peace begins."*
>
> **BARACK OBAMA**

New Student: Liam

78 30-MINUTE GROUPS: **PEACEFUL CONFLICT RESOLUTION**

CHAPTER 8
THE APOLOGY PROCESS: SAYING SORRY AND FORGIVING OTHERS

MIND MAP

Apology – admitting when you are wrong or have done something that caused harm to others and showing remorse or regret for your actions

On the board, draw a Mind Map and ask students to consider the meaning of **Apology.**

Mind Map for Grades 4-9

30-MINUTE GROUPS: PEACEFUL CONFLICT RESOLUTION

- **Saying Sorry** – Saying you're sorry for something you did that hurt someone else
- **Forgiveness** – Choosing to let go of anger and giving someone another chance
- **Responsibility** – Admitting what you did and owning your actions
- **Remorse** – Feeling bad about something you said or did
- **Repair** – Trying to fix the hurt by making things better or right
- **Empathy** – Understanding how someone else feels, especially when they're hurt

Mind Map for Grades 2-3

- **Saying Sorry** – Saying "I'm sorry"
- **Forgiveness** – Letting go of being mad
- **Honesty** – Telling the truth about what you did
- **Regret** – Feeling bad about what you did
- **Fixing** – Trying to make things better
- **Caring** – Thinking about how others feel

ASCA® STANDARDS

- **B-LS 4.** Self-motivation and self-direction for learning
- **B-SMS 1.** Responsibility for self and actions
- **B-SMS 2.** Self-discipline and self-control
- **B-SS 4.** Empathy
- **B-SS 5.** Decision-making and social responsibility
- **B-SS 6.** Effective collaboration and cooperation

DIRECTIONS

- Review the Group Expectations.
- Conduct a student check-in with the Mood Meter.
- Review and discuss the Mind Map.
- Read the Lesson Introduction and ask the Circle Time Questions.
- Read the Story and follow with Discussion Questions.
- Complete the Skill Practice, Would You Rather?, and Additional Activities as time allows.
- Wrap up with the Closing Considerations for each lesson.

In a small group format, conduct your student check-in using the Mood Meter. Ask students to hold up their number (5, 4, 3, 2, or 1) to show the type of day they are having. Validate each student's number and thank them for sharing. If time, you may ask volunteers to elaborate with one reason they chose their number. Ask the group if they have anything to say to be helpful and encouraging to other group members who shared a 1 or 2 for their check-in. Model kind and uplifting responses for the group each week so they can learn how to respond when a group member is having a tough day.

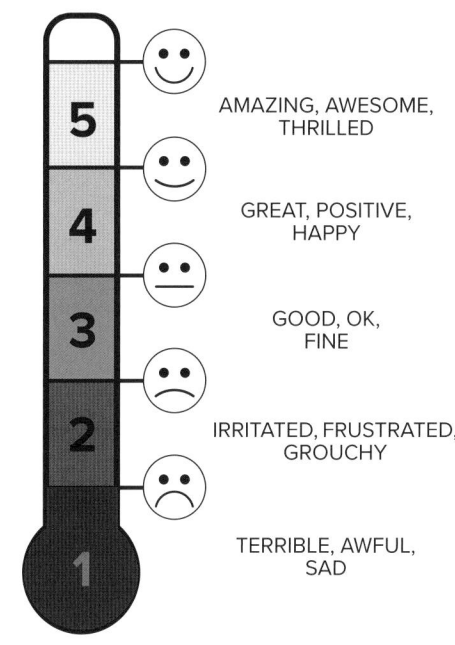

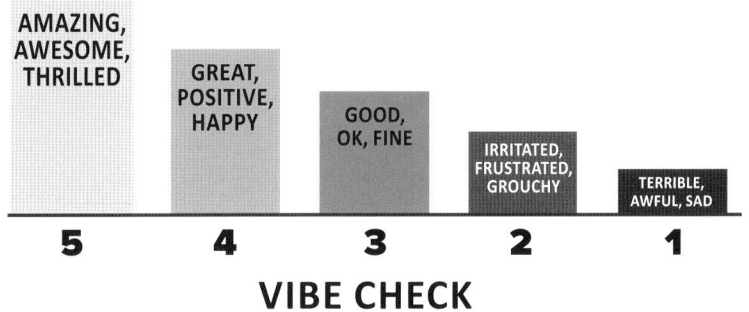

Review the Group Expectations before reviewing the Mind Map. Then, read the Lesson Introduction and ask the Circle Time Questions before reading the Story and the Discussion Questions. Students can work in pairs to craft their responses or share with the whole group. Complete the Skill Practice, Would You Rather?, and Additional Activities as time allows. Be sure to complete the Closing Considerations with each lesson.

LESSON INTRODUCTION

We all make mistakes sometimes—whether it's saying something hurtful, forgetting to help a friend, or not keeping a promise. What can we do when we mess up? How can we fix things when our actions hurt someone else? The answer is what this lesson is about: how to apologize. An apology is a way to say, "I'm sorry" and show that we care about the other person's feelings. It can be very hard to do, but it's an important step in making things right.

Today, we will discuss the apology process, which is more than just saying "sorry." It's about taking responsibility for what happened, understanding how our actions affected others, and finding ways to repair the situation. We'll also talk about forgiveness—how it helps us move forward and why asking for it is just as important as apologizing.

30-MINUTE GROUPS: PEACEFUL CONFLICT RESOLUTION

By learning how to apologize sincerely and forgive others, we can build stronger friendships, create a kinder environment, and solve conflicts peacefully.

CIRCLE TIME QUESTIONS

Ask students to reflect and share their answers to the following questions with the group. Larger groups may need to be broken into smaller groups to give students ample time to share their answers and deepen the conversation.

- Share an example of how you can say you're sorry to someone. What does it mean to say "sorry"?
- Why do you think it can be hard to apologize or forgive others?
- What are some ways you can show someone that you're truly sorry, beyond just saying "sorry"?
- How can apologizing help fix a friendship or relationship?
- What's the difference between an apology and just saying "my bad" or "oops"?

STORY TIME

Hand out the Coloring Sheets and crayons or markers to younger students while the facilitator reads the story, if desired.

Lunchroom Laughter

It was lunchtime, and Carson was walking back to his table, carefully balancing his lunch tray, when his foot caught on a backpack strap. He tried to catch himself, but he tripped and spilled his entire tray—cheese pizza, chocolate milk, and applesauce—all over the front of his shirt.

The room was quiet for half a second … and then the laughter exploded!

Carson's face turned red with embarrassment as he jumped up and looked around at the mess. But the worst part wasn't the spill or the screaming—it was seeing his best friend, Shay, laughing at him with everyone else.

Carson stared at her in disbelief. "Really?" he muttered, hurt flashing across his face before he turned and rushed toward the bathroom.

Shay's smile dropped immediately. She didn't mean to hurt Carson's feelings—she'd just laughed without thinking, but the look on his face made her feel overcome with guilt.

Coach Tyus, who had been monitoring the lunchroom, saw everything. He watched Carson leave the cafeteria with concern, then walked over to Shay, who now looked unsure and uncomfortable.

"Shay," he said, "that didn't look like a great time for either of you. You want to fix it?"

She nodded slowly. "I didn't mean to laugh … but I did. And now he's really mad."

Coach Tyus gave her a reassuring smile. "Sounds like you need to give a real apology. Want to learn a way that can help make it right?"

Shay nodded again.

"It's called the **Four-Part Apology**," he said. "It's not just about saying 'sorry'—it's about taking responsibility and helping the other person know you understand why they're hurt and what you did."

Coach Tyus held up four fingers.

"One: **'I am sorry for...'** You name what happened.
Two: **'It was wrong because...'** You explain why it was hurtful.
Three: **'Next time, I will...'** You share how you'll do better.
Four: **'Do you forgive me?'** You give him the choice to forgive."

Shay listened carefully, then took a deep breath. "Okay. I definitely want to try that."

A few minutes later, Carson came back from the bathroom in a clean shirt from the nurse's office, still quiet and clearly upset. Shay walked over slowly, standing in front of him feeling nervous.

"Carson ... " she said quietly. "I'm really sorry for laughing when you spilled your lunch. It was wrong because I'm your friend, and I should've helped you instead of joining in. Next time, I'll stand up for you and not laugh at you. Do you forgive me?"

Carson looked at her, still a little hurt, but surprised by how honest and sincere she sounded. He thought for a moment, then gave a small nod. "Yeah. I forgive you," he said. "Just ... don't do that again."

"I won't," Shay said quickly. "Promise."

Coach Tyus, watching nearby, gave a small smile and a thumbs-up.

It meant the world to Carson that his friend took the time to not only say sorry for laughing at him, but to also promise to stand up for him next time. He knew he would always do the same for her, too.

DISCUSSION QUESTIONS

- How do you think Carson felt when he saw Shay laughing with everyone else? Why did it hurt more coming from her?
- Have you ever laughed at someone in the moment and then felt bad about it later? What did you do?
- Why do you think it's important to name what you did wrong in an apology, like Shay did?
- Why is important to ask, "Do you forgive me?"
- Do we always have to forgive someone if they hurt or mistreat us? Why or why not?
- How can you use the four-part apology in your own life if you hurt someone's feelings—even by accident?

Using the round-robin method, go around the table and ask students how they would practice each skill, giving everyone a chance to answer one question. You can adapt Skill Practice to allow students to respond in pairs or write their answers on paper.

Using the **Four-Part Apology template**, ask students to write or speak how they would apologize for the following situations:

- You don't invite one friend to your birthday party and the friend finds out.
- You spread a rumor you later find out isn't true.
- You yell at a classmate during a group activity out of frustration.
- You borrow something without asking and return it damaged.
- You push past someone in the hallway and don't say excuse me.
- You make a joke about someone's appearance and realize it hurt their feelings.

ADDITIONAL ACTIVITIES

OPTION 1: "APOLOGY VS. EXCUSE" SORT

Cut out the **Apology vs. Excuse Cards** in advance so students can sort with a partner. Share this lesson:

Sometimes, we struggle to take responsibility for our mistakes. Instead of apologizing sincerely, we use excuses or blame someone else for our own mistakes. In this activity, you will have 10 cards. With a partner, sort which cards fall under the "Apology" category and which cards are "Excuses."

Apology Cards

- I'm sorry for interrupting you. It was wrong because I didn't let you finish. Next time I'll wait my turn. Do you forgive me?
- I'm sorry I took your markers. It was wrong because they weren't mine to use. Next time I'll ask you first.
- I'm sorry I didn't include you in the game. It was wrong because everyone deserves to feel welcome. Next time, you can be on my team.
- I'm sorry for yelling at you. It was wrong because I hurt your feelings, and I'll work on staying calm next time. Do you forgive me?
- I'm sorry I blamed you for something you didn't do. I know that was unfair.

Excuse Cards

- Sorry, but you started it.
- I didn't mean to, so it shouldn't matter.
- It wasn't a big deal. You're overreacting.
- Well, everyone else was doing it, too.
- I only said that because I was mad.
- Sorry, but if you hadn't done that, I wouldn't have …

OPTION 2: FORGIVENESS CIRCLE

This activity is intended to build empathy and create space for honest discussion. Have students sit in a circle. Ask them the following questions and allow them to have an open discussion.

- What makes it hard to forgive someone?
- How do you know when an apology is real?
- Why is beneficial to you to forgive someone who hurt you?
- Pretend someone is this group is a person you know you need to forgive. Role play saying, "I forgive you," and tell them why.

OPTION 3: DEAR _____ APOLOGY LETTER

Students will reflect and write a sincere apology. Have students write a letter to someone (real or fictional) using the four-part apology format. They can share if they want or keep it private as a reflection piece.

CLOSING CONSIDERATIONS

We all make mistakes—it's a part of life and we can learn from them. What matters most is what we do after we make those mistakes. Today, we learned that a real apology is more than just saying, "my bad," or "sorry." It's about taking responsibility, showing empathy, and making a promise to do better next time. If we want to maintain trust, we have to keep our promises.

Using the four-part apology helps us fix hurt feelings and rebuild trust with others. It also reminds us that we all have the power to make things right, even after a mistake. When someone apologizes to us, forgiving them actually helps us let go of anger and move forward with personal peace.

Sincerely apologizing is a small step that can make a big difference. Apologizing and forgiving aren't always easy—but they are always worth it

Ask students to summarize the content of this session's lesson in one sentence.

1. I'm sorry for...

2. This is wrong because...

3. In the future, I will...

4. Will you forgive me?

Apology vs. Excuse Cards

"It wasn't a big deal. You're overreacting."	"Sorry, but you started it."
"I didn't mean to, so it shouldn't matter."	"I'm sorry I blamed you for something you didn't do. I know that was unfair."
"I'm sorry for yelling at you. It was wrong because I hurt your feelings, and I'll work on staying calm next time." Do you forgive me?"	"Well, everyone else was doing it, too."
"I'm sorry I took your markers. It was wrong because they weren't mine to use. Next time I'll ask you first."	"I'm sorry I didn't include you in the game. It was wrong because everyone deserves to feel welcome." Next time, you can be on my team."
"I'm sorry for interrupting you. It was wrong because I didn't let you finish. Next time I'll wait my turn. Do you forgive me?"	"I only said that because I was mad."

"WOULD YOU RATHER?" GAME

Playing the Would You Rather? Game is a fun and engaging activity for students to develop their critical thinking skills. Students will reflect on their experience, evaluate their options based on their preferences, and reflect on the opinions of others, providing a different perspective and strengthening their sense of connection to one another.

WOULD YOU RATHER?

Copy and cut out the questions for small groups to discuss, or have each person stand in the center of the room and move towards one side or the other to show their vote for either option as the facilitator reads the questions aloud.

Would you rather:
- Apologize in front of the class
- Write a private note to the person you hurt

Would you rather:
- Be the first to apologize
- Wait for the other person to go first

Would you rather:
- Have someone who hurt you say I'm sorry and not mean it
- Have someone who hurt you not say anything at all

Would you rather:
- Admit you were wrong and feel embarrassed
- Stay silent and feel guilty

Would you rather:
- Be someone who always says sorry
- Someone who always forgives

Would you rather:
- Fix a friendship after a fight
- Walk away and never talk to that person again

30-MINUTE GROUPS: PEACEFUL CONFLICT RESOLUTION

Boundaries and Balance: Finding Win-Win Solutions to Resolve Problems

MIND MAP

Win-Win Solution – everyone gets something they need, and nobody feels like they lost

On the board, draw a Mind Map and ask students to consider the meaning of **Win-Win Solutions**.

- COOPERATION
- COMPROMISE
- EMPATHY
- Win-Win Solutions
- BOUNDARY
- PERSONAL NEEDS
- ASSERTIVENESS

- **Compromise** – A solution where both sides give up something to reach an agreement
- **Cooperation** – Working together toward a shared goal or solution
- **Empathy** – Understanding and sharing another person's feelings or perspective
- **Boundary** – Rules and limits we set for how others can treat us
- **Assertiveness** – Expressing your needs and feelings clearly and respectfully
- **Personal Needs** – Things that are important to a person's well-being or success in a situation

ASCA® STANDARDS

- **B-LS 4.** Self-motivation and self-direction for learning
- **B-SS 2.** Positive, respectful, and supportive relationships with students who are similar to and different from them
- **B-SS 4.** Empathy
- **B-SS 6.** Effective collaboration and cooperation skills
- **B-SS 7.** Leadership and teamwork skills
- **B-SS 9.** Social maturity and behaviors appropriate for the situation
- **M 2.** Sense of acceptance, respect, support, and inclusion for self and others in the school environment

DIRECTIONS

- Review the Group Expectations.
- Conduct a student check-in with the Mood Meter.
- Review and discuss the Mind Map.
- Read the Lesson Introduction and ask the Circle Time Questions.
- Read the Story and follow with Discussion Questions.
- Complete the Skill Practice, Would You Rather?, and Additional Activities as time allows.
- Wrap up with the Closing Considerations for each lesson.

In a small group format, conduct your student check-in using the Mood Meter. Ask students to hold up their number (5, 4, 3, 2, or 1) to show the type of day they are having. Validate each student's number and thank them for sharing. If time, you may ask volunteers to elaborate with one reason they chose their number. Ask the group if they have anything to say to be helpful and encouraging to other group members who shared a 1 or 2 for their check-in. Model kind and uplifting responses for the group each week so they can learn how to respond when a group member is having a tough day.

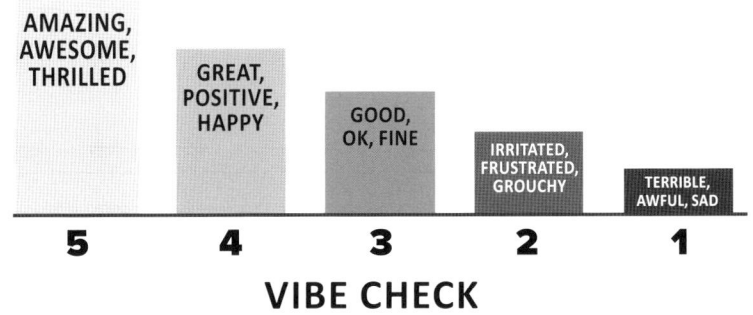

VIBE CHECK

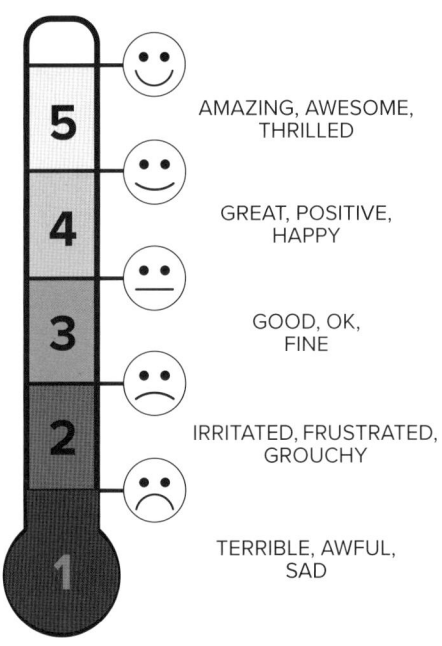

TEMPERATURE CHECK

30-MINUTE GROUPS: PEACEFUL CONFLICT RESOLUTION

Review the Group Expectations before reviewing the Mind Map. Then, read the Lesson Introduction and ask the Circle Time Questions before reading the Story and the Discussion Questions. Students can work in pairs to craft their responses or share with the whole group. Complete the Skill Practice, Would You Rather?, and Additional Activities as time allows. Be sure to complete the Closing Considerations with each lesson.

LESSON INTRODUCTION

In this chapter, we will talk about how setting boundaries and finding balance can help us resolve conflicts in a healthy way. Whether at home, in school, or with friends, disagreements are part of life—but how we handle them makes all the difference. By focusing on win-win solutions, we can find ways where everyone's needs are met, and no one feels left out or like they lost.

We'll also learn the importance of respecting yourself and your own needs to create balance and boundaries during conflicts. We can find ways to work together to reach solutions that benefit everyone, but it should not take away your peace. Whether it's standing up for yourself or listening to others, having clear boundaries is a big part of maintaining healthy relationships or learning to walk away. We teach others how to treat us by what we accept, and not every relationship is good for you. Sometimes it will take courage to find a way to end a relationship. It also takes practice to learn how to find compromise, set boundaries, and create a sense of fairness for all involved.

CIRCLE TIME QUESTIONS

Ask students to reflect and share their answers to the following questions with the group. Larger groups may need to be broken into smaller groups to give students ample time to share their answers and deepen the conversation.

- Can you think of a time where you and a friend or family member came up with a compromise you were both happy with? Please share.
- Do you have a friend that always wants to have it their way? How do you feel about that? Are they being a good friend to you?
- What are some things you could say to a person who doesn't like to compromise or give in to your ideas sometimes?
- Do you find it hard or easy to be assertive about how you feel?

STORY TIME

Hand out the Coloring Sheets and crayons or markers to younger students while the facilitator reads the story, if desired.

Rainforest Resolution

> It was Thursday afternoon in Ms. Becky's class, and the students were working in groups on their "Habitats Around the World" posters. Grayson, Will, and Emma were assigned to work together on the rainforest.

"I'll draw the animals!" Grayson said quickly, grabbing the markers.

"I wanted to do the animals," Will said, frowning. "I already wrote down some cool ones—like jaguars and toucans."

Emma looked up from reading the directions. "I thought we all agreed yesterday that I'd do the drawings."

"No, we didn't!" Grayson said. "I was planning to draw the sloth since we started this."

Will crossed his arms. "It's not fair if Grayson gets to do everything."

Emma sighed. "Now we're just arguing and wasting time."

The three of them stared at the big, blank poster board. It had a title and a green border, but nothing else. Other groups were already halfway done.

Grayson looked around. "We have to decide on something. We only have one more work period before it's due."

Emma had an idea. "What if we *split* the drawings? Like, we each pick two animals to draw?"

Will nodded slowly. "That could work … and maybe we each write a few facts, too. Like a mini-section for each person."

Grayson smiled. "Yeah! We each get to do part of the drawing and the writing."

"And we can help each other color at the end to make it look like one big rainforest," Emma added.

By the end of the class, their poster had monkeys swinging through trees, a jaguar hiding in the leaves, and a big bright toucan sitting on a branch. Each section had a few facts and colorful pictures, and they were all proud of it.

When Ms. Becky came by, she smiled. "Great teamwork, you three. Looks like you figured out how to share the spotlight."

Grayson, Will, and Emma looked at each other and grinned.
"It turned out even better this way," Will said.

"And way more fun," added Emma.

DISCUSSION QUESTIONS

- What was the students' problem in the story and how did they solve it?
- Can you think of any other solutions that would still allow a win-win outcome for all three?
- How did each student contribute to the project?
- How did each student get their personal needs met?
- Why do you think Ms. Becky praised the students at the end?

SKILL PRACTICE

Using the round-robin method, go around the table and ask students how they would practice each skill, giving everyone a chance to answer one question. You can adapt this Skill Practice to allow students to respond in pairs or write their answers on paper.

- Two students on the playground both want to use the same swing. They only have 10 minutes of recess left. How can they make it fair?
- Your group has three members. One wants to use a slideshow, one wants to make a poster, and the third wants to do a skit. What is your solution?
- You're trying to work quietly at your desk, but the student next to you is tapping their pencil loudly. You don't want to get them in trouble. What can you say to be assertive?
- Two friends want you to sit with them at different lunch tables. They both say, "You sat with them yesterday!" How can you handle it to consider everyone's personal needs?
- Your class has a new learning game on the computer. A friend of yours purposely takes your time slot every time it's your turn. What do you say and how do you set a boundary for next time?

ADDITIONAL ACTIVITIES

OPTION 1: YES/NO/MAYBE SORTING ACTIVITY

Using the **Yes/No/Maybe worksheet**, read each statement and decide whether it shows a healthy boundary, an unhealthy boundary, or depends on the situation. Then check the box in the **Yes**, **No**, or **Maybe** column that best matches your opinion.

- It's okay to say no if a friend asks you to share something personal and you're not ready.
- You should always say yes when someone needs help, even if you're overwhelmed.
- Telling someone how you feel when they hurt you is important, even if it's uncomfortable.
- You should ignore your own needs if someone else is upset.
- Taking a break from a friendship that feels one-sided is okay.
- You should forgive someone if they say they are sorry the first time they hurt your feelings.

OPTION 2: TALK IT OUT ROLE PLAY

Put students in pairs and give each pair one a scenario to read through and plan their role play. They can put on a skit or sit back-to-back and act like it is a phone conversation. After each pair completes their role play, discuss the takeaways as a class.

- Student one is doing all the work in a group project while the others aren't helping.
  Parts: Student one wants to speak up without causing drama. Student two is not helping.
- Friend one keeps asking to borrow things— phone, homework, lunch money—and Friend two is starting to feel uncomfortable but doesn't want to hurt feelings.
  Parts: Friends one and two

- A sibling or caregiver keeps pushing you to do things when you need a break. You want to ask for time alone without being rude.
  Parts: Pushy sibling/You asking for space

- A group of friends is pressuring you to go along with something that doesn't feel right (e.g., gossiping, breaking a rule). You want to say no but still stay friends.
  Parts: Friend trying to convince you to break a rule/You are saying no in a respectful way

- Student one keeps messaging you late at night and expects instant replies. Student two wants to set a digital boundary while keeping things friendly.
  Parts: Student 1/Student 2

OPTION 3: BOUNDARY MAP

Using the **Boundaries Map worksheet**, have students create a visual "boundaries map" showing different areas of their lives (school, family, friends, online). In each area, they list one healthy boundary they want to keep or set, and why it's important.

CLOSING CONSIDERATIONS

Today we've learned how setting healthy boundaries and finding win-win solutions can help us resolve conflicts in a peaceful way while also taking care of our emotional well-being. Disagreements at home, school, and with friends are going to happen, but how we handle them can lead to positive outcomes for everyone. When we set clear boundaries, we protect our own needs and create a space for respectful communication. Setting boundaries isn't about shutting others out—it's about creating healthy, respectful relationships where everyone's needs are valued.

When we compromise, we try to find win-win solutions so everyone feels like they end up with something they need. With practice, you can learn to resolve conflicts in ways that result in understanding, compromise, and positive solutions for all.

Ask students to summarize the content of this session's lesson in one sentence.

Yes/No/Maybe

Read each statement below and decide whether it shows a healthy boundary, an unhealthy boundary, or depends on the situation. Then check the box in the Yes, No, or Maybe column that best matches your opinion.

	YES 👍	NO 👎	MAYBE ❓
It's okay to say no if a friend asks you to share something personal and you're not ready.	☐	☐	☐
You should always say yes when someone needs help, even if you're overwhelmed.	☐	☐	☐
Telling someone how you feel when they hurt you is important, even if it's uncomfortable.	☐	☐	☐
You should ignore your own needs if someone else is upset.	☐	☐	☐
Taking a break from a friendship that feels one-sided is okay.	☐	☐	☐
You should forgive someone if they say they are sorry the first time they hurt your feelings.	☐	☐	☐

Boundaries Map

Each circle below represents an area of your life (school, home, family, friends, online, and a blank one to add your own.) In each area, list one healthy boundary you want to keep or set and why it's important.

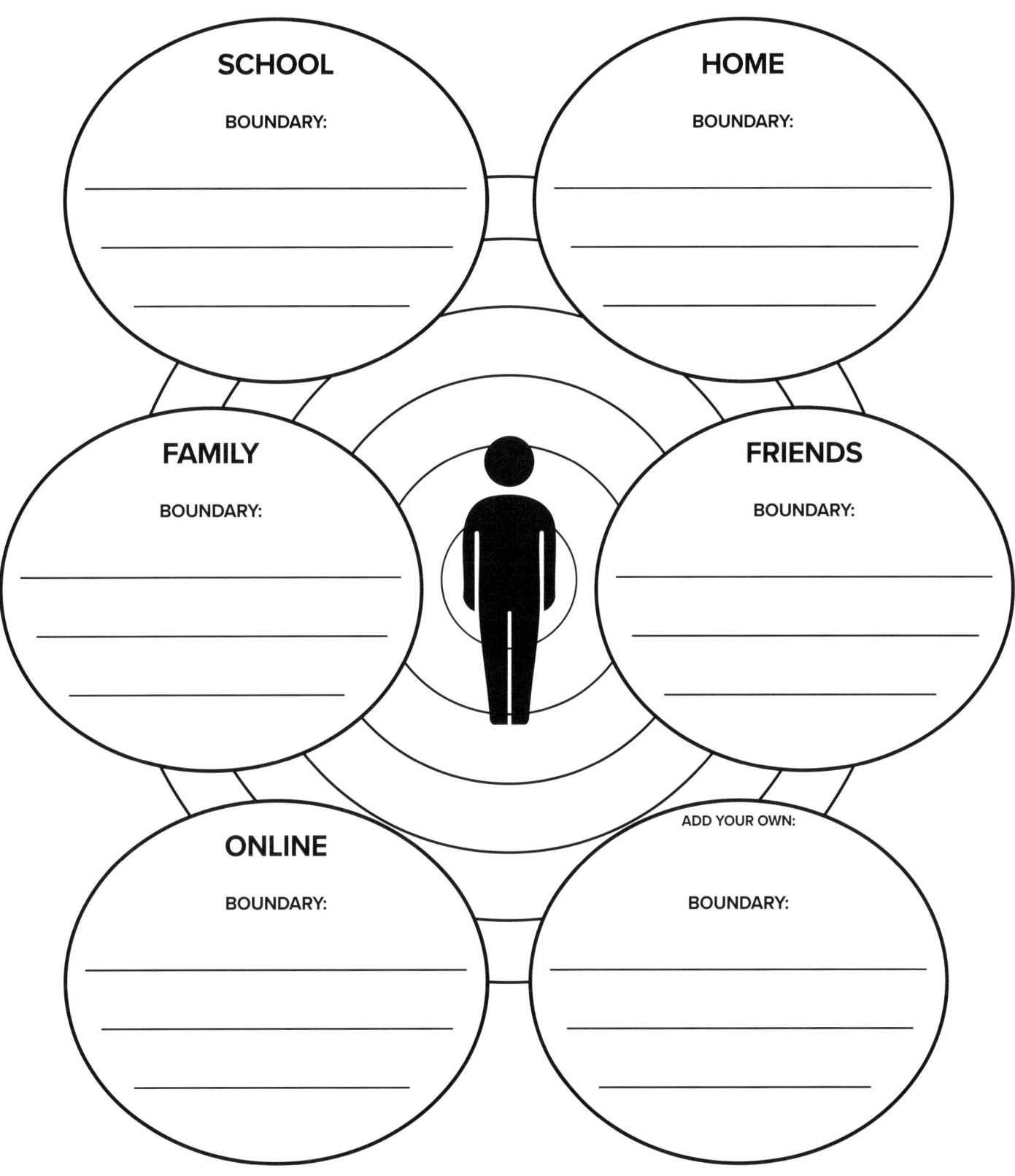

"WOULD YOU RATHER?" GAME

Playing the Would You Rather? Game is a fun and engaging activity for students to develop their critical thinking skills. Students will reflect on their experience, evaluate their options based on their preferences, and reflect on the opinions of others, providing a different perspective and strengthening their sense of connection to one another.

Would You Rather?

Copy and cut out the questions for small groups to discuss, or have each person stand in the center of the room and move towards one side or the other to show their vote for either option as the facilitator reads the questions aloud.

Would you rather:
- Speak up for yourself in a disagreement
- Stay silent to avoid conflict

Would you rather:
- Walk away from a hurtful friendship
- Try to work things out one more time

Would you rather:
- Give in to keep the peace
- Try to find a win-win where both sides are happy

Would you rather:
- Say no to protect your own time and energy
- Say yes to make someone else happy

Would you rather:
- Set a boundary that might upset someone
- Avoid the topic to keep things easy

Would you rather:
- Let a small issue go to avoid drama
- Talk it out to clear the air

30-MINUTE GROUPS: **PEACEFUL CONFLICT RESOLUTION**

PEACEKEEPING IN ACTION: BEING KIND AND RESPECTFUL TO SOLVE PROBLEMS PEACEFULLY

MIND MAP

Peaceful Problem-Solving — finding a way to fix or solve a disagreement without hurting others

On the board, draw a Mind Map and ask students to consider the meaning of **Peaceful Problem-Solving**.

Mind Map for Grades 4-9

- CALM
- CONSIDERATE
- COMPROMISE
- COOPERATIVE
- COLLABORATIVE

PEACEFUL PROBLEM-SOLVING

The Five C's of solving problems peacefully:

- **Calm** – choosing helpful words and using a neutral or quiet tone of voice
- **Considerate** – thinking about another person's feelings during a dispute
- **Cooperative** – working together so each person's individual goals are understood and valued
- **Collaborative** – working together to achieve shared goals (Win-Win)
- **Compromise** – a way to reach an agreement where each participant gives up something they want to end the dispute

Mind Map for Grades 2-3

```
    CALM                    CARING
         \                /
          PEACEFUL
       PROBLEM-SOLVING
         /      |       \
   FAIR DEAL  WORKING   TEAMWORK
              TOGETHER
```

- **Calm** – Stay cool and use kind words and a quiet voice
- **Caring** – Think about how the other person feels
- **Teamwork** – Help each other and listen to everyone's ideas
- **Working Together** – Work as a team to find a solution that makes everyone happy
- **Fair Deal** – Both people give a little to solve the problem

ASCA® STANDARDS

- **B-LS 4.** Self-motivation and self-direction for learning
- **B-SMS 1.** Responsibility for self and actions
- **B-SMS 2.** Self-discipline and self-control
- **B-SMS 7.** Effective coping skills
- **B-SS 2.** Positive, respectful and supportive relationships with students who are similar to and different from them
- **B-SS 6.** Effective collaboration and cooperation skills

DIRECTIONS

- Review the Group Expectations.
- Conduct a student check-in with the Mood Meter.
- Review and discuss the Mind Map.
- Read the Lesson Introduction and ask the Circle Time Questions.
- Read the Story and follow with Discussion Questions.
- Complete the Skill Practice, What Would You Do – This or That, and Additional Activities as time allows.
- Wrap up with the Closing Considerations for each lesson.

In a small group format, conduct your student check-in using the Mood Meter. Ask students to hold up their number (5, 4, 3, 2, or 1) to show the type of day they are having. Validate each student's number and thank them for sharing. If time, you may ask volunteers to elaborate with one reason they chose their number. Ask the group if they have anything to say to be helpful and encouraging to other group members who shared a 1 or 2 for their check-in. Model kind and uplifting responses for the group each week so they can learn how to respond when a group member is having a tough day.

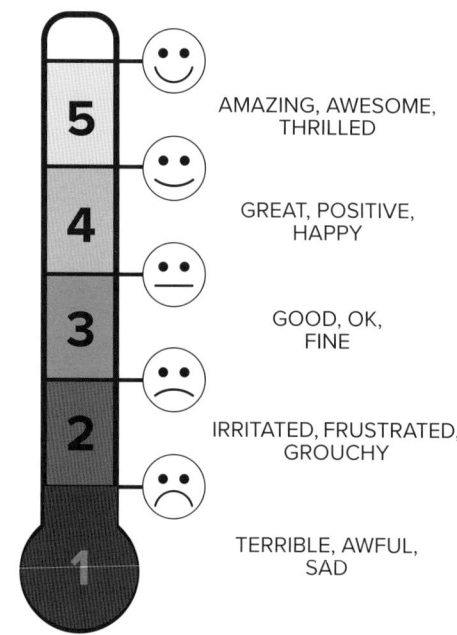

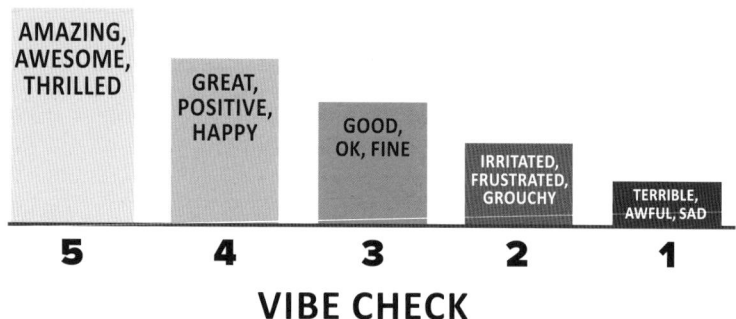

Review the Group Expectations before reviewing the Mind Map. Then, read the Lesson Introduction and ask the Circle Time Questions before reading the Story and the Discussion Questions. Students can work in pairs to craft their responses or share with the whole group. Complete the Skill Practice, What Would You Do - This or That, and Additional Activities as time allows. Be sure to complete the Closing Considerations with each lesson.

LESSON INTRODUCTION

We have spent several weeks together learning many different skills we can use to solve problems peacefully. Today's lesson is about putting it all together, in the heat of the moment, when we face problems with others.

When you use the **Five C's** to solve a problem, it helps everyone feel safe and respected. It can calm things down and make it easier to decide on your solution.

Being kind doesn't mean you have to say yes to everything. It means you listen, use nice words, and show you care about how others feel—even if you don't agree.

Our final goal is to use the skills we've learned—like staying calm, listening carefully, using respectful words, apologizing when needed, setting boundaries, and finding win-win solutions—in our real-life situations. Solving problems peacefully takes practice, but every time we try, we get better at it. You've been working on it; now go do it!

CIRCLE TIME QUESTIONS

Ask students to reflect and share their answers to the following questions with the group. Larger groups may need to be broken into smaller groups to give students ample time to share their answers and deepen the conversation.

- Why do you think showing kindness and respect are important when solving a problem with someone?
- Can you think of a time when someone was kind or considerate to you during a disagreement? How did it make you feel?
- What does being respectful look or sound like during an argument or conflict?
- Is it possible to disagree with someone and still treat them kindly? How?

STORY TIME

Hand out the Coloring Sheets and crayons or markers to younger students while the facilitator reads the story, if desired.

Group Chat Challenges

The moment Kiera opened her phone after school, she felt her stomach drop.

The group chat with her friends—Lexia, Bryson, and Tori—was blowing up with angry messages. What started as a disagreement about weekend plans had quickly turned rude and personal.

Bryson: "You always want to do what *you* want. You don't listen to anyone else."

Tori: "Wow. Just say you don't want me there."

Lexia: "Forget it. I'm done trying to make everyone happy."

Kiera stared at the screen. She liked all of them, and they usually got along, but something about this weekend had made everything explode. She took a breath and typed:

Kiera: "Can we all take a second and cool off? This is starting to sound more like fighting than figuring stuff out."

There was a long pause.

Lexia: "I guess I got defensive. I just felt like no one cared if I came or not."

Tori: "I didn't mean it like that. I just thought a movie night would be chill. I didn't know you had something else in mind."

Bryson: "Yeah, we could've just said it differently. Sorry I snapped."

Kiera smiled. The whole mood had shifted. No one was rude, no one went silent—just a few honest, respectful replies.

Kiera: "Maybe next time we can all say what we want *before* the plans get made. We're all trying to have fun—we don't have to get so mad when it's not exactly like we want."

Later that evening, Lexia messaged her privately:

Lexia: "Thanks for calming everyone down. I was ready to just leave the group."

Kiera: "You're welcome. It's easier to talk when no one's feeling attacked."

Lexia responded with a smiley face and a heart. Things weren't perfect, but they were back on track—and this time, with a little more kindness.

DISCUSSION QUESTIONS

- What helped the group go from arguing to having a respectful conversation?
- How did Kiera show kindness and respect even though she wasn't part of the argument?
- Why do you think people sometimes say hurtful things during disagreements, even to friends?
- What could have happened if no one had spoken up the way Kiera did?
- Have you ever been in a similar situation with friends? What could you do next time to solve the problem peacefully?

SKILL PRACTICE

Pass out the **What Would You Say? worksheet**. Using the round-robin method, go around the table and ask students how they would practice each skill, giving everyone a chance to answer one question. Ask students to write down examples of what they would say in each situation and then share with the group.

- You're working on a group project, and one classmate keeps taking over and not listening to anyone else's ideas. Another group member is getting frustrated and stops participating. How can you use the five C's to speak up respectfully, include everyone, and keep the project moving forward peacefully?
- Two of your friends are arguing about whose turn it is to use the classroom computer. They both want you to take their side. What peacekeeping skills can you use to stay calm, avoid choosing sides, and help your friends come to a fair agreement?
- You make a joke in class, but someone takes it the wrong way and gets upset. They accuse you of being mean. How can you use respectful words and listening skills to explain your side, apologize if needed, and help both of you move on in a positive way?

- You and your friends planned to sit together at the whole school assembly, but one friend accidentally gets left behind and is upset. What could you say or do to show consideration and include your friend again? How can you repair the situation and make sure it doesn't happen again?
- A friend keeps telling your private business to another friend, even after you've said don't do it. How can you set clear boundaries and use peaceful communication to solve this problem without creating drama?

ADDITIONAL ACTIVITIES

OPTION 1: PEACEKEEPER ROLE PLAY CARDS

Students form a circle. One student volunteers to step into the middle and role play a conflict scenario with a classmate. After the short scene, the class suggests ways to use the five C's to resolve the issue. Then, the scene is replayed with the new approach.

OPTION 2: FIVE C'S POSTERS/SLIDESHOW

Students create posters or slides for a slideshow that show the five C's with drawing/graphics, examples, and phrases they can use in real-life situations.

OPTION 3: KIND WORDS RELAY

In teams, students race to write out as many kind, respectful, or calming phrases as they can think of that could be used during a conflict (Ex. "I understand how you feel," "Can we find a solution?"). The team with the most phrases written in two minutes "wins." Reflect on how these phrases change the tone of a disagreement.

Younger students can say them instead of writing them.

*OPTION 4: PEACEKEEPER CHALLENGE CHART

This is the final activity and is recommended.

Over the next two weeks, students are challenged to use the chart to track moments when they use a peacekeeping skill—like staying calm, listening, or compromising. At the end of week two, they are asked to drop the chart off to the counselor/teacher who led the group for a certificate or treat.

- Stayed calm during a conflict with a peer
- Listened without interrupting
- Used respectful words even when annoyed/angry
- Showed empathy or kindness to someone
- Did not talk back to an adult even when frustrated
- Found a win-win solution
- Walked away from a heated conflict

- Apologized sincerely to a friend/family member
- Used "I" statements to express feelings
- Set a boundary calmly
- Willingly gave up something and found a compromise
- Helped others solve a disagreement peacefully

CLOSING CONSIDERATIONS

Today is our last formal meeting as a group to learn about *Peaceful Conflict Resolution*—but it is not over! Your work as a peacekeeper and peacemaker starts now. Throughout our weeks together, you've learned many skills to help you handle conflicts in ways that are calm, respectful, and fair. You've practiced staying in control of your emotions, listening with empathy, speaking up kindly, setting healthy boundaries, and working toward solutions that help everyone feel heard and safe.

In this final chapter, Peacekeeping in Action, you learned how to put all those skills together in real-life situations. Peaceful problem-solving isn't about being perfect or avoiding disagreements. That truly is not possible as conflict is a part of our human experience. It's about choosing to treat others with respect—even when it's hard—and trying to work things out in a way that helps everyone feel safe and valued.

Please remember:

- Don't let others steal your peace. Every time you stay calm, you build inner strength.
- Pause, Process, Proceed. Every time you stop and listen with care, you build trust.
- "Peace begins with a smile." -Mother Teresa. Every time you act kindly and seek solutions, you build peace.

You now have the skills to be a true peacekeeper in your classroom, your friendships, your family, and anywhere you go. Keep practicing, keep learning, and keep choosing peace. You are ready.

Go make a difference!

Ask students to summarize the content of this session's lesson in one sentence.

What Would You Say?

Write examples of what you would say in each situation and share your answers with the group. Remember the 5 C's: calm, considerate, cooperative, collaborative, compromise.

1. You're working on a group project, and one classmate keeps taking over and not listening to anyone else's ideas. Another group member is getting frustrated and stops participating.

How can you use the five C's to speak up respectfully, include everyone, and keep the project moving forward peacefully?

___

2. Two of your friends are arguing about whose turn it is to use the classroom computer. They both want you to take their side.

What peacekeeping skills can you use to stay calm, avoid choosing sides, and help your friends come to a fair agreement?

___

3. You make a joke in class, but someone takes it the wrong way and gets upset. They accuse you of being mean.

How can you use respectful words and listening skills to explain your side, apologize if needed, and help both of you move on in a positive way?

___

4. You and your friends planned to sit together at the whole school assembly, but one friend accidentally gets left behind and is upset.

What could you say or do to show consideration and include your friend again? How can you repair the situation and make sure it doesn't happen again?

___

5. A friend keeps telling your private business to another friend, even after you've said don't do it.

How can you set clear boundaries and use peaceful communication to solve this problem without creating drama?

___

30-MINUTE GROUPS: PEACEFUL CONFLICT RESOLUTION

Peacekeeper Challenge Chart

	DATE	SCENARIO	DATE	SCENARIO
Stayed calm during a conflict with a peer				
Listened without interrupting				
Used respectful words even when annoyed/angry				
Showed empathy or kindness to someone				
Did not talk back to an adult even when frustrated				
Found a win-win solution				
Walked away from a heated conflict				
Apologized sincerely to a friend/family member				
Used "I" statements to express feelings				
Set a boundary calmly				
Willingly gave up something and found a compromise				
Helped others solve a disagreement peacefully				

"WHAT WOULD YOU DO - THIS OR THAT?" GAME

Playing the What Would You Do - This or That? Game is a fun and engaging activity for students to develop their critical thinking skills. Students will reflect on their experience, evaluate their options based on their preferences, and reflect on the opinions of others, providing a different perspective and strengthening their sense of connection to one another.

WHAT WOULD YOU DO-THIS OR THAT?

Copy and cut out the questions for small groups to discuss, or have each person stand in the center of the room and move towards one side or the other to show their vote for either option as the facilitator reads the questions aloud.

What would you do if someone cuts in front of you in line?
- Speak up calmly and ask them to move back
- Stay silent but feel angry the rest of the time

What would you do if your friend says something that hurts your feelings?
- Tell them honestly how it made you feel
- Keep it inside and stop talking to them

What would you do if a classmate blames you for something you didn't do?
- Defend yourself respectfully and explain your side
- Blame them back and start an argument

What would you do if you're really angry during a disagreement?
- Take a deep breath and wait before responding
- Say the first thing that comes to mind

What would you do if you made a mistake and hurt someone's feelings?
- Apologize sincerely and try to make it right
- Pretend it didn't happen and hope they get over it

What would you do if a group you want to hang out with said your friend can't join?
- Invite the left-out person to hang out with just you
- Stay quiet so you don't lose your chance to be in the group

30-MINUTE GROUPS: PEACEFUL CONFLICT RESOLUTION

Final Group Session

LAST SESSION:
Directions & Overview

This final session is recommended, but optional. You may conclude the group during the final lesson topic if time does not permit this final session.

Directions: This final session is more relaxed and carefree, allowing students to spend time with one another and process their feelings about the group's conclusion. Facilitators may provide structured games or allow students unstructured time together.

Post-Group Expectations: Many students will have grown accustomed to meeting with you and will need reassurance about what support will be available after the group's conclusion. Be sure to review the protocol for meeting with you once the group has concluded.

Pre- and Post-Group Assessment: Ask students to complete the Post-Group Assessment. Review the directions aloud. Discreetly ensure that all the questions were answered when the forms are returned.

Certificate of Completion: Present each student with their own Certificate of Completion. You can have as much or as little fanfare around this experience as you would like. Playing a song and asking students to stand and clap for their peers creates lasting memories for the participants.

Group Completion Letter: Give each student their Group Completion Letter to share with their caregiver, notifying them that the group has officially ended.

Group Conclusion: Ask each student to share what, if anything, this group has meant to them. Model this activity by sharing your experience as the group's facilitator.

Note to Facilitators: If your district allows, concluding a group with a meal is often a fun experience for the students. If you are unable to purchase a meal with the district budget, perhaps students could bring their lunches. Be sure to have caregiver permission and be familiar with student allergies before providing students with any food.

ACTION PLAN

GRADE LEVEL
The curriculum is ideal for 2nd through 9th grade students.

GROUP TOPICS
Understanding Conflict: Differences and Disagreements

Conflict Resolution Styles: Understanding How We Manage Disagreements

The Power of Words: How to Communicate Respectfully

Active Listening: The Key to Understanding

Nonverbal Communication: What Are You Really Saying?

Finding Calm: Strategies for Managing Strong Emotions

Empathy in Action: Walking in Someone Else's Shoes

The Apology Process: Saying Sorry and Forgiving Others

Boundaries and Balance: Finding Win-Win Solutions to Resolve Problems

Peacekeeping in Action: Being Kind and Respectful to Solve Problems Peacefully

10-12 Sessions — 30 MIN

Curriculum:
Use this *Peaceful Conflict Resolution* Workbook to facilitate your groups.

Materials:
Copies of the Surveys, Coloring Sheets, What Would You Do – This or That?/Would You Rather?, Activity printouts, crayons, pencils, and scratch paper.

Small group is ideal for 8-10 students. Fewer students may be optimal if students with more severe behaviors are included.

Peaceful Conflict Resolution can also be used for classroom lessons.

ASCA® STUDENT BEHAVIOR STANDARDS 15

B-LS 4	B-SS 4
B-LS 9	B-SS 4
B-SMS 1	B-SS 5
B-SMS 10	B-SS 6
B-SMS 2	B-SS 7
B-SMS 7	B-SS 9
B-SS 1	M 2
B-SS 2	

ASCA® MINDSETS AND BEHAVIOR DATA

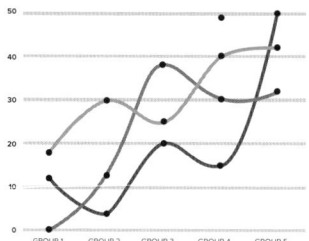

Use *Peaceful Conflict Resolution* assessment data to create a visual representation of their progress using their pre- and post-data.

OUTCOME DATA

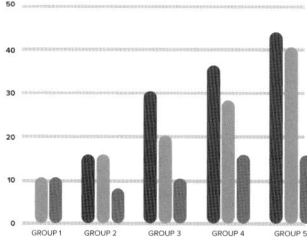

Use achievement, attendance, and discipline data to measure your students' progress. Compare the pre- and post-data to answer the question "how did the learning affect student outcomes?"

PEACEFUL CONFLICT RESOLUTION GROUP PERMISSION FORM

Greetings, Caregivers of: _____,

This form invites your student to attend a **Peaceful Conflict Resolution Group**. Our counseling department offers various services, including class lessons, small groups, and individual sessions with students. There are many different reasons we invite students to attend groups.

We invite students who might need help connecting with their peers, managing conflict or big emotions, improving their grades, or simply because their involvement will allow them to be more successful in their education journey. Your student is not in trouble, and being part of this group is meant to be a positive time for all attendees.

This group will focus on strengthening communication skills, fostering cooperation with peers and adults, and resolving disagreements peacefully. We will also address managing stress and emotions during conflicts so your student feels more confident in handling difficult situations both in school and outside of school. Small groups are a safe way for students to learn valuable skills and connect with peers.

We will meet for approximately thirty minutes during the school day _____ times per week. I will work with your child's teacher to select an appropriate time that minimizes interruptions to their learning. When the student has completed all the group sessions, they will receive a Certificate of Completion.

I am excited to work with your child. Please don't hesitate to contact me with any questions or concerns.

Warm regards,

Please complete and return by: _____

Student's Name: _____

Teacher's Name: _____

☐ YES, I agree to allow my child to attend the Peaceful Conflict Resolution Group.

☐ NO, I do NOT agree to allow my child to attend the Peaceful Conflict Resolution Group.

_____
Signature of Caregiver

PEACEFUL CONFLICT RESOLUTION GROUP EXPECTATIONS

CONFIDENTIALITY

In our group, we will keep what we talk about confidential. Confidentiality means keeping what is said in the group private and not discussing it outside of the group. We know that some things are private, and not everyone needs to know about them. However, because we are a group, we can't promise that everyone will keep what you say private, so please be mindful of what you share with the group. If you share that you plan to hurt yourself or someone else or that someone is hurting you, I will keep you safe, but telling someone who needs to know can help keep you and others safe as well.

SAFETY

We create an environment of physical and emotional safety. We don't make fun of anyone, laugh at anyone, and we watch out for each other. What else do you think we should do to keep our group safe?

ASK FOR HELP WHEN NEEDED

This is a safe place to ask questions and receive help.

LISTEN TO EACH OTHER

Listen from your heart. This is a space to be open, truthful, and respectful. Everyone belongs and everyone will have a turn. When others are speaking, we will listen with our full attention.

HELP OTHERS WHEN WE CAN

It is okay to disagree, but we won't yell or call each other names. We can support each other in keeping this group and this time together safe, helpful, and respectful.

DO OUR BEST

When we fully commit to listening and participating respectfully, we will get more out of the group and grow stronger with the important skills of listening, self-control, cooperation, and solving conflicts.

CREATE YOUR OWN

_____

_____

Group Attendance Form

Group:_____ Day/Time:_____

	1	2	3	4	5	6	7	8	9	10	11	12
DATE												
	☐	☐	☐	☐	☐	☐	☐	☐	☐	☐	☐	☐
	☐	☐	☐	☐	☐	☐	☐	☐	☐	☐	☐	☐
	☐	☐	☐	☐	☐	☐	☐	☐	☐	☐	☐	☐
	☐	☐	☐	☐	☐	☐	☐	☐	☐	☐	☐	☐
	☐	☐	☐	☐	☐	☐	☐	☐	☐	☐	☐	☐
	☐	☐	☐	☐	☐	☐	☐	☐	☐	☐	☐	☐
	☐	☐	☐	☐	☐	☐	☐	☐	☐	☐	☐	☐

SESSION 1

SESSION 2

SESSION 3

SESSION 4

SESSION 5

SESSION 6

SESSION 7

SESSION 8

SESSION 9

SESSION 10

SESSION 11

SESSION 12

Group Attendance Form (Example)

Group: 5th Grade Lunch **Day/Time:** Thursday@12:30

	1	2	3	4	5	6	7	8	9	10	11	12
DATE	3/2	3/9	3/16	3/23								
Jane/Ms. W's Class	X	X	X	X	X	X	X	X	X	X	X	X
George/Mr. Day's Class	X	X		X	X	X	X	X	X	X	X	X
Sami/Ms. Smith's Class	X	X	X	X	X	X	X	X	X	X	X	X
John/Ms. Lee's Class	X		X	X	X	X	X	X	X	X	X	X
Malik/Ms. Lee's Class	X	X	X		X	X	X	X	X	X	X	X
Prishna/Ms. Smith's Class	X	X	X	X	X	X	X	X		X	X	X

SESSION 1	Intro/Assessment/Group Rules and Norms/Discussed expectations/Played game.
SESSION 2	Understanding Conflict: Differences and Disagreements
SESSION 3	Conflict Resolution Styles: Understanding How We Manage Disagreements
SESSION 4	The Power of Words: How to Communicate Respectfully
SESSION 5	Active Listening: The Key to Understanding
SESSION 6	Nonverbal Communication: What Are You Really Saying?
SESSION 7	Finding Calm: Strategies for Managing Strong Emotions
SESSION 8	Empathy in Action: Walking in Someone Else's Shoes
SESSION 9	The Apology Process: Saying Sorry and Forgiving Others
SESSION 10	Boundaries and Balance: Finding Win-Win Solutions to Resolve Problems
SESSION 11	Peacekeeping in Action: Being Kind and Respectful to Solve Problems Peacefully
SESSION 12	Check-ins/Assessment/Process group experience & Certificates awarded.

Pre- and Post-Assessment

My name is:_____

Date:_____

Peaceful Conflict Resolution Assessment

Circle 👍 if the statement is **true** for you.

Circle 👎 if the statement is **NOT true** for you.

There are no right or wrong answers!

I know how to stay calm when I'm in an argument.	👍	👎
I try to listen to the other person's side during a disagreement.	👍	👎
I understand that not every disagreement has to turn into a fight.	👍	👎
I understand what it means to set a boundary with someone.	👍	👎
I try to solve problems without yelling or blaming.	👍	👎
I know when to walk away from a conflict.	👍	👎
I can think of more than one way to solve a problem with someone.	👍	👎
I ask for help from an adult when I can't solve a conflict on my own.	👍	👎
I know the difference between being assertive and being aggressive.	👍	👎
I try to work together with others even when we don't agree.	👍	👎
I believe that everyone's voice should be heard during a conflict.	👍	👎

Anything else you would like to share about the group? Write it below.

_____

_____

Results Report
Peaceful Conflict Resolution Assessment Data

GROUP GOAL:

STUDENT STATEMENTS:

Academic Results
Increase the total Benchmark scores/Reading Level following group intervention for group participation by ____%

____%

Attendance Results
Decrease the number of absences by ____% following group intervention for group participants

____%

Discipline Results
Decrease the number of conduct referrals by ____% following group intervention

____%

STUDENTS ATTENDED

NUMBER OF SESSIONS

OVERALL IMPROVEMENT

(See Formula Lower Right)

☐ Pre-Assessment % True ☐ Post-Assessment % True

- I know how to stay calm when I'm in an argument.
- I try to listen to the other person's side during a disagreement.
- I understand that not every disagreement has to turn into a fight.
- I understand what it means to set a boundary with someone.
- I try to solve problems without yelling or blaming.
- I know when to walk away from a conflict.
- I can think of more than one way to solve a problem with someone.
- I ask for help from an adult when I can't solve a conflict on my own.
- I know the difference between being assertive and being aggressive.
- I try to work together with others even when we don't agree.
- I believe that everyone's voice should be heard during a conflict.

OVERALL IMPROVEMENT FORMULA

$$\left(\frac{\text{Post-Assessment Total} - \text{Pre-Assessment Total}}{\text{Pre-Assessment Total}}\right) \times 100$$

Results Report (Example)
Peaceful Conflict Resolution Assessment Data

GROUP GOAL:

Reduce the number of minor or major referrals for fighting or aggression toward other students or staff by 20% for students who had more than three discipline referrals last year.

STUDENT STATEMENTS:

"I liked meeting with this group."
"Everyone treated each other respectfully when we met together."
"I know how to solve conflicts in a more peaceful way by talking or compromising."
"We were able to practice what we learned during the group meeting as well as outside of the group."
"I know how to choose my words carefully during an argument."
"I know how to assess my body language so I give the message I want to give."

Academic Results
Increase the total Benchmark scores/Reading Level following group intervention for group participation by __5__%

__5__%

Attendance Results
Decrease the number of absences by __30__% following group intervention for group participants

__30__%

Discipline Results
Decrease the number of conduct referrals by __33__% following group intervention

__33__%

STUDENTS ATTENDED: 6

NUMBER OF SESSIONS: 12

OVERALL IMPROVEMENT: 63.15%
(See Formula Lower Right)

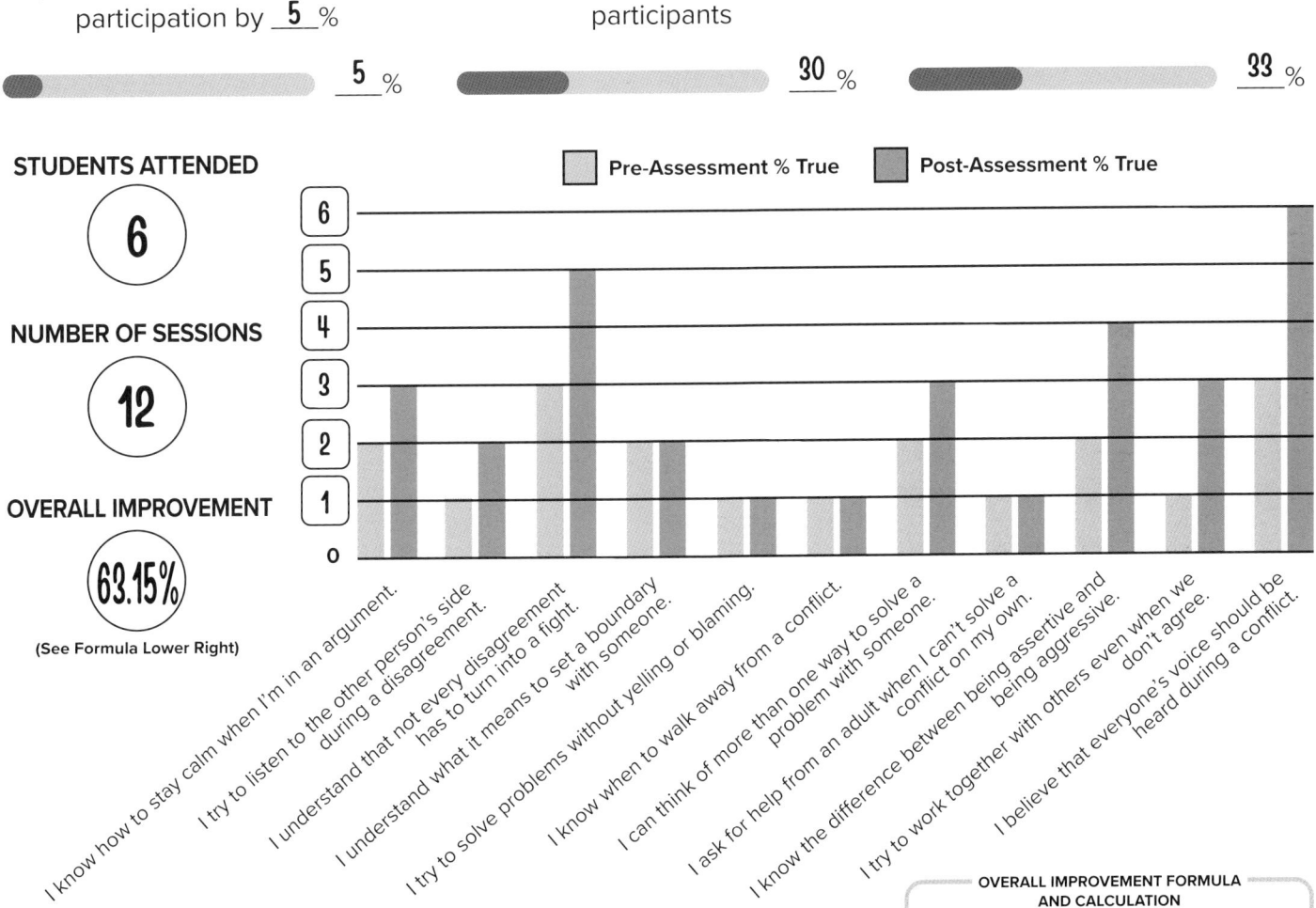

OVERALL IMPROVEMENT FORMULA AND CALCULATION

$$\left(\frac{\text{Post-Assessment Total} - \text{Pre-Assessment Total}}{\text{Pre-Assessment Total}}\right) \times 100$$

$$\left(\frac{31-19}{19}\right) \times 100 \quad (.6315) \times 100 = 63.15\%$$

30-MINUTE GROUPS

CERTIFICATE OF COMPLETION

This Certificate is Presented to:

_____

For Participating in the **Peaceful Conflict Resolution Group!**

Facilitator: _____

WELL DONE!

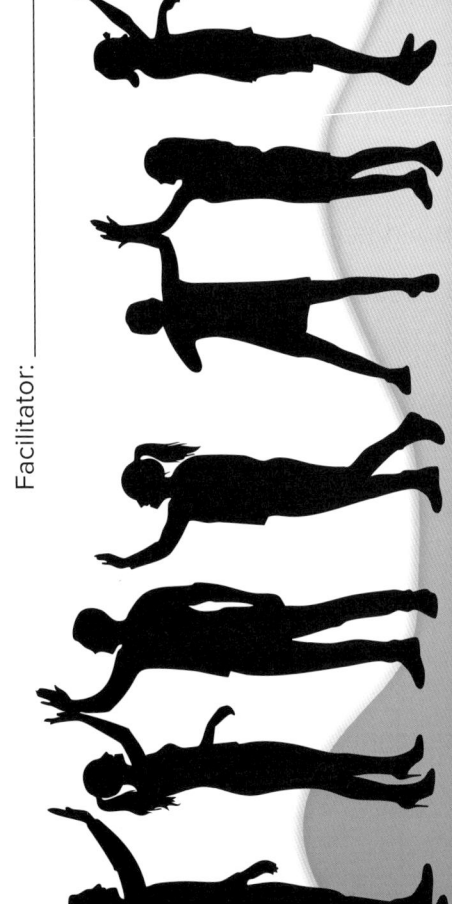

PEACEFUL CONFLICT RESOLUTION GROUP COMPLETION LETTER

Date:_____

Hello!

Today was the final session in our Peaceful Conflict Resolution Group, and we wanted to let you know that your student has been presented with a Certificate of Completion.

Over the past ten sessions, we have reviewed the following topics:

- Understanding Conflict: Differences and Disagreements
- Conflict Resolution Styles: Understanding How We Manage Disagreements
- The Power of Words: How to Communicate Respectfully
- Active Listening: The Key to Understanding
- Nonverbal Communication: What Are You Really Saying?
- Finding Calm: Strategies for Managing Strong Emotions
- Empathy in Action: Walking in Someone Else's Shoes
- The Apology Process: Saying Sorry and Forgiving Others
- Boundaries and Balance: Finding Win-Win Solutions to Resolve Problems
- Peacekeeping in Action: Being Kind and Respectful to Solve Problems Peacefully

Your student has had the opportunity to learn, discuss, and practice many skills taught each week, and I am so hopeful about their continued progress with our support. Please ask them to share a few skills with you that they have learned and will continue to focus on for their own personal growth.

I am still their counselor and will still be available to them as needed. However, we will no longer be meeting each week. Please don't hesitate to contact me with any questions or concerns.

I am so proud of them and excited they were able to attend. Thank you so much for allowing them to participate in our Peaceful Conflict Resolution Group!

Warm regards,

_____
School Counselor

ENDNOTES

1. https://www.mtdtraining.com/blog/thomas-kilmann-conflict-management-model.htm)

Sayadat, Nazmus. (2024). Review The Thomas Kilmann Conflict Resolution Model: What Lesson for Organizational Conflict Management can be Drawn from this Model?. 10.13140/RG.2.2.17893.41445.

THE RESOURCES IN THIS BOOK ARE AVAILABLE FOR YOU AS A DIGITAL DOWNLOAD!

Please visit **ncyi.org/downloadable-resources** to access the downloadable resources.

Enter the code below to unlock the resources:

RESOLUTION592

ABOUT THE AUTHOR

Connect with Amie at www.behaviorqueen.com

Amie Dean, M.ED., B.A. has worked in education since 1993. She has experience teaching at all levels, and has taught both special and general education. She was with Fulton County Schools (GA) for ten years, where she provided support to teachers and students as the Student Support/RTI Coordinator for her middle school for four of those years. She holds a Master's degree in Education, is Nationally Board Certified as an Exceptional Needs Specialist, and has trained with Dr. Rick DuFour, Dr. Kay Burke, Dr. Spencer Kagan, Dr. Ruby Payne, and many others. Amie was also certified as a trainer for The World of Difference Institute with the ADL and studied Restorative Circles which helped hone her practice in coaching students and educators with problem solving, communication, and peacekeeping skills. With decades of experience as an educator and a professional consultant, she now provides support to others through training, speaking, and writing. Amie is also the author of many books, including Because You Believe in Me, Your Happy Heart, There's No Dream Too Tall, and 15-Minute Focus: Behavior Interventions: Strategies for Educators, Counselors, and Parents and accompanying Workbook.

Amie's Sessions

Behavior Interventions That Work

Do you have a plan for what you will do when a student doesn't comply with your request the first time? Second time? How about the third time? Do you go home tired and exhausted from frustration? This presentation will guide you in developing a thorough, preventative plan for handling issues from low level distractions to serious/chronic behaviors. This is a practical, hands-on presentation filled with concrete steps you can use the next day to help students and yourself.

Motivating Challenging Students

Like many of you, I have had classes, and often students, which led me to think, "How will I make it this year?" I have spent my career as a classroom teacher searching for and learning which strategies work with students. My only criteria: positive and practical! This session is designed for teachers who believe that every student has a gift to offer the world. We have to find ways to help them realize it.

Social/Emotional Literacy in the Classroom

Do your teachers have strategies for building respectful learning communities in their classrooms? How can they help students feel the 3 C's – Connected, Capable, and Contributing without giving up too much instructional time? In this session, participants will be introduced to two methods that are proven to build positive classroom communities – Responsive Classroom and Tribes.

Creating Trauma-Sensitive Classrooms

In today's classrooms, more and more students are living in or recovering from trauma and chronic stress. Many educators feel overwhelmed and unprepared to deal with the behaviors that are a result of these situations children are facing. This session will provide participants with concrete strategies that can be implemented in classrooms to support students by building relationships, trust, and teaching coping strategies.

About NCYI

National Center for Youth Issues provides educational resources, training, and support programs to foster the healthy social, emotional, and physical development of children and youth. Since our founding in 1981, NCYI has established a reputation as one of the country's leading providers of teaching materials and training for counseling and student-support professionals. NCYI helps meet the immediate needs of students throughout the nation by ensuring those who mentor them are well prepared to respond across the developmental spectrum.

Connect With Us Online!

@nationalcenterforyouthissues

@ncyi

@nationalcenterforyouthissues